For Mikaal, Zaynadin and Hanaa.

*May these words help you navigate
your own paths in life.*

Contents

Introduction

The fortieth birthday had a lot to answer for. At a time when I thought I could reasonably expect a degree of stability, certainty and confidence in the way my life was progressing, it seemed I was destined for anything but. Despite almost twenty years practising as a barrister specialising in criminal law, and having to stand up and "perform" in court, almost on a daily basis, here I was, racked with self-doubt, and feeling wholly unsure as to the direction my life was heading. The career, which twenty years earlier seemed to almost guarantee a rosy future, had, by now, been rocked by a series of moves by successive governments, which had the effect of undermining the independent Criminal Bar to such an extent that barristers with formerly healthy practices, were now actively pursuing alternative career paths. It became increasingly common to hear of colleagues who were leaving to join the Crown Prosecution Service, or defence solicitors' firms as in-house advocates. Those who could turn their hands to other areas of the law, such as civil or family, began to swap the cut and thrust of criminal advocacy for the regular work available in other (albeit much duller) fields.

The uncertainty surrounding work was accompanied by the onset of recent family responsibilities. My record-breaking (at least for Muslims) resistance to tying the knot was a somewhat amusing achievement at the time, but seemed less funny now that I was a forty-year-old who shared responsibility for running around after two small children. The energy levels seemed to be diminishing and, along with a rapidly expanding bald patch, served as a constant reminder that perhaps my best days were firmly behind me, and, that the future was going to involve no more than struggling to keep up with the children, pay the bills, and generally just get by (like most normal people, in fact). I began to reminisce about missed opportunities, and how my three monastic years at university may well have propelled me heavenward, but were not memorable for much else. Since then I had lived off the kudos that came with being a barrister, but had hardly set the legal world ablaze with my talents, fearing instead that each day may hold the moment when I would finally be "found out". So, rather than diving enthusiastically into the pool of life, I had, in fact, spent most of mine paddling around the shallow end.

If all this sounds typical of a mid-life crisis, then I could at least take heart from the fact that many a mid-life crisis has been the source of a re-birth or re-invention of oneself. As a Muslim, I found it not without relevance, that even our beloved Prophet Muhammad (peace be upon him), was destined to carry out his most significant work after the age of forty. So there was hope that perhaps the best was yet to come. There were undoubtedly things that I could do, and do well. For the last ten years or so, I had been delivering talks on Islam, which had been well received. They were hardly of the academic variety, but the years of addressing juries had clearly helped in enabling me to establish a rapport quite easily with an audience, and that soon emerged as my USP. It was all the more important because it soon transpired that meeting a fairly normal kind of guy who just happened to be a Muslim, was evidently not something that many of the audiences were used to. It was also important work because it took place at a time when it was very much needed.

The tragic events of the 11th September 2001 inevitably meant that Muslims faced a stark choice. They could attempt to keep their heads down and just try to live their lives, pretty much as the older generation had done since the 1960s and '70s. Alternatively, they could meet the challenges they faced, and attempt to address the concerns that the general public now had about Islam and its adherents. Many people were questioning why it was that we did not hear from the "moderate" Muslims. Others wanted to know if such people even existed. Islam became increasingly portrayed as an alien religion that had nothing to do with "our Judaeo-Christian values", and there was a sudden proliferation of so-called experts willing to opine on what Muslims really believed.

Sadly, however, these experts were too often not Muslims themselves, and, in some cases, even had their own ulterior motives to advance. It was against this background that I figured that any advocacy skills I might possess could hardly be used for a more worthy cause than trying to dispel myths about my faith, and so, I began accepting any invitation that came along to speak about Islam. Obviously, I regarded myself as a moderate Muslim, certainly as opposed to an extremist one, but I was also concerned about the definition of "moderate Muslim". Did it really mean the overwhelming majority of Muslims I knew who did not practice or condone intolerance and violence, or did it simply mean those who were compliant and not given to rocking any boats? These were questions that I needed answering for myself, as well as for others.

For me, speaking about Islam went hand in hand with developing good relations with those of other faiths. Unlike some of my fellow Muslims, I did not believe that people who followed other faiths simply existed in the anticipation of one day receiving information about Islam. They were individuals and communities who had their own hopes and fears, talents and abilities, and, perhaps most importantly, their own humanity. Getting to know one's fellow human beings, just for the sheer sake of it, is not optional for Muslims but is, rather, a duty derived from the Quran itself. Happily it was not exactly a new experience for me to speak to people outside the Muslim community, but, perhaps even I underestimated just how much I could learn from them as I soon discovered that one of the incidental benefits of becoming involved in inter-faith work was having contact with people who actually thought about their religious beliefs. Believers, who attempted to understand their faith and ponder its practical implications in their daily lives, were notable by their absence in the Muslim communities with which I came into contact. Yet, on the inter-faith scene there was an abundance of such people, and this, I felt, could only be an enriching experience. There seemed to be a depth to their religious experiences from which I felt that some Muslims, myself included, should be learning lessons.

At a mundane level, ordinary Muslims are undoubtedly good at the ritual observance part of their faith. I believe that many are deeply impressive when one looks at their sincere and genuinely held beliefs, and these are qualities, which cannot, and should not, be under-estimated. However, we are not living in a religious age, but, rather, an age when religious belief is constantly challenged, undermined or simply side-lined. It is no longer sufficient to have a genuine faith and regular ritual observance if one's peer environment expects more. Muslim communities, perhaps more than most, can reasonably be expected to have their beliefs placed under the microscope in a society which seeks answers, and is prepared to carry out the investigations which may unearth them. In order to answer the questions being posed it is simply not good enough to adopt an "Islam is the solution" stance, particularly when usually we do not even know what the problem is for which we are proposing this "solution". It may be that there is, in fact, little wrong with certain societies as compared to others. If our basic needs are met and we live in relative security, then these facts have to be acknowledged, and we should not compare our situation to societies where such comforts are absent. What we need to do, first and foremost, is ask whether or not Islam is simply intended for the moral instruction of individuals, or, whether it has a role to play for wider society. If, as suggested here, the latter is true, then we must understand our society and its needs. It is only then that we can begin to think about the message of the Quran, and consider how it may be put to practical use.

It may well be that Islam can offer a solution to the problems posed by materialist consumerism. There may be a spiritual void in the lives of individuals, which needs to be filled. There may be gross economic injustices for individuals, as well as for society at large, which need alternative solutions to those which are currently being tried and which seem only to perpetuate the cycles leading to inevitably disastrous consequences. The Islam that may have answers to these problems and others, is, in my view, not the Islam being practised by so many of its followers today. Although ritual observance is impressive and, indeed, necessary, on one level, on another it is a poor replacement for actually thinking about one's faith and, in particular, how to adapt it to modern life. Indeed, not thinking about one's faith runs contrary to so many injunctions of the Quran itself.

It was no accident that adaptations or accommodations between the faith and the realities of life were a common feature of early Islam. Since that "golden age", however, a rigidity has set in whereby Muslims are led to believe that all the necessary thinking has been done, and now the path to salvation simply consists of following the existing rules. Little effort has been made to update, or reform, such rules, and, as a result, it is Muslims themselves who suffer first and foremost. It is a sad indictment of the level of thinking taking place in many Muslim communities that the very mention of the word "reform" draws the ire of so-called scholars, and, therefore, in turn, the rest of the masses. The constant revisiting of the faith which is necessary to keep it relevant, and which was such a common feature in Islamic history, is now confused with diluting the faith in order to please the non-believing West.

It would seem that religion is not going to naturally wither away as many of its critics had assumed. It had previously been regarded as inevitable that the evolution of enlightened thought would eventually lead civilised people to discard the "primitive" religious baggage, which they had been carrying around for millennia. Religion was just another phase of development that humanity would outgrow on its evolutionary path, and a time would come when "pure" thinking, unfettered by superstition, would hold sway over the world. How shocking it must be, therefore, to those who held that view, to witness the resurgence of religious thought, which began in the latter part of the last century. It would perhaps have been understandable if such a resurgence was restricted to less developed societies which had failed to progress, and, therefore, had to conceal their shortcomings behind a veil of religion. Often, such societies are characterised by an aversion to any criticism of the way they are administered, and, religion, therefore, provides a useful device to restrict such criticism, and control populations which may be inclined towards independent thought. The fact remains, however, that this religious resurgence has not been limited to such underdeveloped societies but, rather, has taken a deep hold even in the liberal, educated, sophisticated West.

I believe that Islam has much to offer this world. Whether or not that is done by those born into the faith, or those who see it with the objectivity of onlookers, remains to be seen. What is plain, however, is that this faith will have to reconnect with its moral essence and become relevant again and, in order to do this; issues of reform will have to be addressed. It is encouraging to note the long-term concerted plan of countries such as Turkey, to revisit their religious texts and re-interpret them in the light of 21st century thinking, but this exercise needs to be extended to other countries and other scholars. If this is not done, then the danger is that literalist, out-dated interpretations of religious texts will continue to dominate, and the result will be a hollow, formal, ritualistic Islam that serves neither Muslims nor the rest of humanity. The only people to benefit will be those who insist on portraying Islam as monolithic and obscurantist, and their Muslim counterparts who have vested interests in maintaining the religious status quo.

In order to prevent this occurring, the debate, which is presently restricted to highbrow academic circles, needs to be joined by all Muslims. Much can be learned from the likes of Tariq Ramadan and others, but such intellectual approaches may not appeal to ordinary Muslims. Perhaps this book can play a small part in bringing some elements of that debate to the Muslim masses. Perhaps it can contribute to reassuring non-Muslims that there is some thinking taking place in the Muslim world and it is of the constructive and enlightened variety. Perhaps all it can achieve is to shed some light on the life of one particular Muslim who is trying his best to reconcile his own faith with the needs of his modern lifestyle.

Whatever it may achieve, as ever, all praise is due to the Almighty, with only the mistakes belonging to us.

CHAPTER 1

The Seventies

If ever a car summed up England in the 1970s it was the Mark III Ford Cortina as driven by DCI Gene Hunt in the original BBC series *Life on Mars,* later to develop into *Ashes to Ashes.* Some may argue with that proposition and suggest that it was, in fact, the Consul/ Granada featured in *The Sweeney,* but Granadas were too big and posh, despite being used by Regan and Carter to capture all manner of London villainy. There are undoubtedly going to be supporters of the Capri and Escort RS2000 made famous in *The Professionals,* but the boys of CI5 were clearly a cut above the rest of us (more like trainee James Bonds actually) and were, therefore, expected to drive flash motors. Bodie's Capri may be remembered fondly as a throwback to the seventies but it was simply too flash to truly symbolise that decade, and Doyle's RS2000 was even more exclusive. Many a young lad growing up in the seventies in Britain will have aspired to one day owning a Capri or an RS2000 but it was the Ford Cortina (grandfather of the Mondeo for younger readers) which was the more likely to be owned by his dad (unless, of course, he happened to be Asian but we shall come to that later).

The Cortina was for the ordinary British working class and for many years Ford felt it appropriate to make it look as plain and ordinary as its likely customers. The original Mark I may have had a restrained elegance about it but its successor could have been designed by any 12-year-old with a ruler. The Mark IV which was to see in the 1980s, however, was proof that Ford could also draw upon the talents of primary school children, as its preponderance of straight lines made even the Volvos of the day look alluringly curvaceous. All this left the Mark III head and shoulders above the rest because it was, quite simply, stunning. It had the right combination of straight lines and curves to signify purpose and elegance and none more so than the GXL model circa 1973. Twin headlights gave it a sporting menace and the initials themselves made it sound like it meant business. In the '80s Gene Hunt may well have said "Fire up the Quattro" but ten years earlier he would have just uttered "GXL" to inspire his footsoldiers in their pursuit of the bad guys.

Yes, there were the later 2.0E and GT models but it was the GXL that impressed me most, not least because my uncle owned one. White may well be the new black at the moment, but, in 1976, it was just another boring colour for cars, and one that was likely to get very dirty very quickly given the general grubbiness of that decade. A white GXL, however, complete with black vinyl roof was the ultimate in cool and while every other Asian family we knew owned either a Toyota or a Datsun (now Nissan), my uncle was "rolling" in a Ford complete with automatic transmission, which in those days was about as *Starsky and Hutch* as you could get. At last he could return to hero status for me after a brief abdication of his responsibilities whilst he had a green Morris Marina.

So there you have it, one of the highlights of that decade for a very young me was cruising the mean streets with my uncle in a white GXL. The mean streets of where, exactly, you may be wondering. Well, any glamour ends there, because we are not talking about the showbiz glitz of, say, London of the '70s. In fact, we are not even talking about a city or even major town up north. No Manchester or Liverpool just yet. Instead the scene is set in a place called Brierfield, situated in East Lancashire, between Burnley and Nelson, not far from Pendle Hill. It was a small place, even now its population is less than 10,000, but to a 6-year-old it might as well have been a big city. It was also home to my immediate family, wider relations and many friends. One of my mother's brothers lived 50 yards in one direction while the other lived further afield, possibly as far as 100 yards away. Streets upon streets of terraced houses starting at the bottom of the hill, near the farms and the railway station, gradually worked their way up the hill to the more "affluent" parts of the town. (It is worth noting that the distance from the bottom of the hill to the top was probably little more than a mile). It seems ridiculous looking back on it now but at the time we had managed to "progress" a good way up the hill and, in fact, secured our social status amongst the community by being the furthest up the hill out of all the Pakistani families who lived there. Progress indeed. (Funnily enough the Pakistani family who lived nearest also shared a similar outlook to us and had the same aspirations to gain an education and make the most of the opportunities afforded to them in their adopted home. They had a son who was my pal but I had little idea then that he would end up marrying my sister over 20 years later, in fact long after we had left the area. I was even less aware that he would go on to become Britain's first Muslim Member of the European Parliament.) It was also perhaps befitting that we lived all the way up there given my father's role in the community.

Mohammad Din Chaudhry had arrived from Pakistan in 1962 with a bag of clothes and a law degree from Peshawar University. Having spent a brief amount of time in London and Nottingham, he decided to move north where work was guaranteed and properties were cheaper, knowing that he would have to buy a house in due course before calling over the rest of the family from their village in the north-east of Pakistan. In the '60s there were plenty of factories in Lancashire offering work but this would only be a short-term measure as he was clearly capable of greater things having been the only person in his whole district in Pakistan to have gained any meaningful education, let alone graduated from university. He was an only child and his mother had died when he was a very small infant. His father was one of three brothers who owned some land, not enough to make them very wealthy but enough to command the most respect in their village. Of the three brothers, two worked the land whilst the third was in the army. It soon became apparent to my grandfather that his son had abilities that would be wasted if he were to remain farming the land. Besides, this was not strictly necessary as my grandfather had a brother and nephews, all of whom were doing this work anyway, so he decided to let his son go and live with the third brother whose army posting meant that he lived away from the village and in a town which had a school. Fortunately, my father made the most of this opportunity, excelled at school and managed to go to university when all around him were resigned to a rural life which required little in the way of formal education.

Having obtained his law degree, on his arrival in England his intention was to become a barrister, thereby following in the footsteps of Mohammed Ali Jinnah, the founder of Pakistan, and Mohammed Iqbal, the great poet of the Indian subcontinent and inspiration behind Jinnah. Grand ambitions for a talented man, but, ambitions, which did not make any allowance for the contracting of tuberculosis that hospitalised him for several months. When he did re-emerge from hospital a career at the Bar no longer seemed so inviting. It has always been a precarious existence and, for my father, newly in the country and recently recovering from illness, it simply posed too many problems, not least because it would have required regular attendance at the Inns of Court in London. He did, however, appreciate that he had to enter a profession and so it was that he began to study to become a teacher.

In the 1960s the Pakistani community in East Lancashire consisted almost entirely of single males who originated from villages in the Punjab area of Pakistan. They had initially come to England with the sole purpose of working, sending money back home, and then ultimately returning there themselves. They could not boast an education, but the jobs they took on did not require one. They were manual labourers, factory workers who slotted into working shifts whilst out of the house and sleeping shifts whilst in. I recall being told stories of how the terraced houses had none of the luxurious but useless clutter, which we have become accustomed to today, but simply contained beds and wardrobes to fulfil the basic functions required. The beds were vacated by the day shift only to be immediately occupied by those returning from a night's work. Any money earned was intended to be sent back home but gradually these same workers decided to have their family members join them, which, in turn, meant spending money on buying property here. Initially it was other male family members who joined them but soon wives were called over too.

This process of sponsoring family members, as well as other tasks necessary to simply get by in England, all required the filling out of official forms. It was not a task that these young men were equipped for and so they had to find someone who could help. It seems that my father's life at the time was divided between work, study, and providing translating services to those that needed them. (On my father's death in 1999 one of his old friends came to pay his respects. I remembered him from my childhood but had not seen him for some 20 years following his move to Scotland. He fondly recalled how he would make arrangements with my father to go out when they were not working. As he was the one with the car he would call round to pick my father up but said that he would get frustrated, because, just as they were about to leave the house, another person would arrive, asking that my father help him fill out a form. He, in turn, would never refuse so they invariably got delayed. Apparently there was only one other man in the locality who could assist with the filling out of these forms but as he charged a fee it was my father who was the more prevailed upon.)

By the late 1960s my father had been joined by my mother and three of her brothers. Initially they all lived together but pretty soon my uncles bought their own homes leaving space for the arrival into this world of myself and my two younger sisters.

My recollection of the early '70s is understandably vague but I do remember being fascinated by cars from a very early age. This interest (or obsession) now looks like it will remain with me for the rest of my life although even I suspected, and perhaps hoped, that I would grow out of it. My mother reports incidents which even I cannot recall, such as the time when one of my father's friends called round to see him but he was not at home so he offered to take me for a ride in his car until my father returned. No sooner had he suggested this than I was in his car and we were off. After a while my mother began to worry and, somewhat belatedly perhaps, began to think that she did not in fact know this individual particularly well at all. Needless to say she was panicking by the time my father returned, but he calmly assured her that there was nothing to worry about, and I was duly brought back safe and sound. Although I do no remember this particular incident, I do recall that my heroes at the time were any of my dad's friends who had cars.

The Pakistani community had already begun to evolve by the 1970s and the very same men, who began their lives in England as factory workers, now began to display an entrepreneurial spirit that remains very much alive today. Although the community in East Lancashire was predominantly from a rural background in Pakistan and, therefore, instinctively less inclined to become involved in business, some clearly saw the opportunities that were on offer and were attracted by the control they could exert over their own fortunes. One business, which remains as attractive now, as it was then, was mini-cabbing. The idea of being able to work as many hours as humanly possible, have a greater control over your life and get cash in your hand is perhaps even more attractive to immigrants than it is to others. Whether or not that is an accurate appraisal, mini-cabbing was certainly attractive to young Pakistani men in the 1970s who wanted to escape the monotonous shift work of the factories and mills and it was not long before they began to set up their own minicab firms. One such firm was Goldline Taxis, which was set up in Nelson around 1976, and although that was the year that we moved away from the area, the memory of that firm serves as a reminder of how the Pakistani community lived at the time.

It was set up by a Pakistani man who, unlike many around him, wanted to move beyond the factories here, and farming back home, and start a business. He had the advantage of belonging to a family that possessed an intriguing dynamic, combining humility and respect with Godfather levels of machinations and violence. He was the second oldest of four brothers, the eldest of whom was a patriarchal figure who happened to be one my father's best friends. This eldest brother had been involved in an accident at his workplace, as a result of which he lost a couple of fingers. Inevitably he had a claim for compensation, which required the filling out of official paperwork so he approached my father for assistance. This was provided as usual in return for no remuneration, the difference being that on this occasion it was provided to someone who did not forget a favour.

Many people had their forms completed by my father and disappeared back to their everyday lives but Mohammed Sharif was made of different stuff. He may have been completely uneducated but he possessed a personality that commanded the respect of all who met him. Despite coming from a simple rural background he had contacts in Pakistan which went all the way up to the higher echelons of government and it was evident from the reactions he aroused in people that although he spoke softly, there was likely to be a big stick not too far away. It would be unfair to suggest that violence played a large part in his daily life, but, as with many men of power, it was an option, which was available to him in a way in which it simply was not for regular people. It was over a decade later, in the mid-'80s, when he was shot dead in Pakistan, that I learned that such power often comes at the expense of making enemies along the way.

To me he was an "uncle", a friend of my father's who was utterly gentle with children, and indeed, anyone I saw him with. He was also an individual whose company my father seemed to enjoy and that required a little more understanding. I have very vivid recollections of accompanying my father to Uncle Sharif's house in Nelson. It was a two-up two-down terraced house that was occupied at the time by Sharif and one of his younger brothers. On the rare occasion that I visit such dwellings now I am surprised at how small they really are. When I was a child, however, they were just normal houses but some of them could certainly pack in the "uncles". I remember Uncle Sharif's house in particular because it seemed to be the place where the most people congregated. The tiny sitting rooms were full of uncles and smoke, although there appeared to be a respectful curtailing of the chain-smoking in the presence of my dad. Cups of tea were regularly brought through from the kitchen and food at appropriate intervals. The most abiding memory I have though, was of the incessant conversation. Hours would pass by while the men talked and talked. As a child, I was inevitably bored and restless, but I was never one of those children who fell asleep easily, preferring instead to remain constantly awake just in case I might miss something, (a trait which I seem to have passed on to my own children). Little did I realise that some elements of those conversations would remain with me forever.

Our family belong to the Gujjar caste. Although on the face of it Islam is supposed to be egalitarian, with no preference being afforded to one group over another, in reality this is an often-contravened ideal. According to the tenets of our faith, it is only our God-consciousness or righteousness, which should distinguish us from each other, but life on the Indian subcontinent was not so clear-cut. There, Islam had to reach accommodations with the Hindu way of life in which the caste system featured prominently. Many of these accommodations can be seen in the Pakistani culture, which, often, has just as much of an Indian Hindu flavour about it, as it does specifically Islamic. Food, dress, language and the caste system all reflected the interwoven lives of Muslims, Sikhs and Hindus on the subcontinent. If anything, changing one's faith was a relatively straightforward matter as compared to doing anything about the immobility of the caste into which one was born. My father never made a big issue of our caste but I still managed to glean that there was a great pride that we were born Gujjar rather than into any other caste. (No doubt other castes may feel the same way and I am certainly not qualified to comment on the relative merits of them all, but, on balance, it is probably a good thing that this particular feature of our culture is fading. After all, some may reasonably argue that we have enough to deal with without complicating our lives further with caste considerations.)

In East Lancashire in the 1970s such caste loyalties still played a significant role. Unlike now, money did not seem to impress people particularly and those who gathered at Uncle Sharif's house certainly did not talk about it. Material possessions did not seem to matter as all the conversations were about respect and honour. Most of the people who congregated there were, in fact, Gujjar and, rightly or wrongly, they felt that their caste was the epitome of such qualities. Gujjars were supposed to be men of respect and valour, integrity and honesty, (and if the truth be told, perhaps a tendency to throw punches first and ask questions later). They were also relatively simple folk, a bit unreconstructed actually, maybe even a bit "Yorkshire". (As for Gujjars from Yorkshire, well...). The conversations, therefore, consisted of much regaling of tales of Gujjar heroism, and some good-hearted mockery of friends who had the "misfortune" of being from other castes.

The one feature that stands out all these years later, however, is the relative absence of religion from those conversations. Nowadays it is an inescapable feature of conversation in Muslim households, often depressingly so given that topical religious issues rarely seem to be associated with good news, but back then being Muslim was almost incidental to being a Pakistani to outsiders, and a Gujjar to those within the community. The battles, literally, that were had with the National Front were nothing to do with their "fear" of Muslims, as their equally repugnant BNP descendants today claim, but were simply because they fancied some "Paki-bashing". Among Muslims in that area there just did not appear to be any major discussion of global politics in a way that so animates them today and clearly the types of conversation reflected the general attitudes prevailing in that community.

It was a community which was certainly Muslim but in an almost "Christian" way. Just as the common criticism of Christians was that they had turned their religion into a once-a-week ritual, so, too, the Pakistani community of East Lancashire was happy to observe occasional religious rituals but certainly could not be described as allowing Islam to inform the way it lived its daily life. Perhaps part of it was due to the fact that it was still a very new community on these shores. Most of the Pakistani inhabitants of Brierfield had arrived in the previous decade or so, and were still very much concerned with the basics of setting up home here. That primarily involved jobs, houses, schools and, admittedly, a place to pray, but as nobody appeared to object to them practising their faith, there really was not much to get excited about on the religious front.

There were no hijabs or niqabs. Funny clothes and even funnier facial hair (at least on the men) did not cause outrage, although that may well have been because they were a common feature of the seventies. There were no Members of Parliament who, now that they were no longer in need of Muslim votes, blubbered about feeling intimidated by the clothes that their female Muslim constituents wore, although again, maybe Lancastrian politicians in the seventies were made of sterner stuff. Newspapers did not carry the now almost daily debates about whether Islam is compatible with "British values". It is tempting to think that perhaps there were no international events in those days that had the effect of thrusting Muslims into the headlines the way they do now, but that patently cannot be correct. The oil crisis of 1973 clearly had the Western world in a panic and it was undoubtedly due to decisions taken by people who happened to be Muslims, but, unlike today, there did not seem to be a pervading requirement that all Muslims in Britain should explain themselves, well, not in East Lancashire anyway.

My own initiation into the faith appeared to be taking the usual path with me being sent to mosque, aged about five, to take part in classes to learn how to read the Quran. The usual path was disturbed, however, when I returned home from my first lesson to announce that there was no way I was going back to the mosque. I had been used to a fairly relaxed household where I seemed to be progressing well without anybody having to scare the life out of me. I was regarded as reasonably bright and my father's interest in education meant that he was never going to leave mine just to the school system. He would tutor me and my sisters from an early age and it soon became apparent that, out of the three of us, I needed the least supervision. It came as something of a shock, therefore, when I went to my first class at the mosque. For a start, despite my father's involvement in the community,

I do not recall having many Pakistani friends at an early age, so, at the mosque, I was out of place as soon as I walked through the door. Added to that, the system of learning by rote, with the maulvi (imam) sitting at the head of the group wielding a big stick, did not exactly fill me with a desire to master Arabic.

Upon hearing my announcement, my father understood that this particular style of "teaching" may not have suited me, so he was content for me to learn Quran at home with daily tuition from him or, more often, my mother. The happy result of this was that I managed to "finish" the Quran, i.e. read it from beginning to end in Arabic, by the age of six when most of those at the mosque achieved the same by the age of 12. I clearly remember the achievement being regarded as an almost barmitzvah-like rite of passage, and getting marked by proud celebrations. In those days, having one's children learn to read the Quran was the only real interest in Islam displayed by the Pakistani families around us. In fact I do not even recall seeing the daily prayers ever being performed at anyone's house, including ours, so religion really did seem to be incidental to the rest of life.

All this was to change, however, after November 1976. That was when we moved from our East Lancashire backwater to the city of Liverpool, which although only 56 miles away, might as well have been the other end of the country as far as our family was concerned. For the previous couple of years my father had been working in Liverpool in a particularly satisfying job teaching English to foreign students at Crown Street Language Centre. His routine of staying there during the week and returning home at weekends was only intended to be a temporary arrangement, but, he soon realised that Liverpool was where he would rather bring up his children. It was an astonishing decision at the time. After all, he would be moving away from all his family and friends to a place where he hardly knew anybody. Not only that but he would be going from being a big fish in a small pond to quite the opposite. I can actually remember people trying to dissuade him and attempting to appeal to him by suggesting that the community would struggle without him.

As ever he knew best. For a start the community was now reasonably well established and in any event, all he had done for them was a bit of translating, hardly life or death stuff. More importantly, however, he had correctly assessed the relative merits of the educational facilities available to his children in Liverpool as compared to those in Brierfield. He realised that if he stayed his children could succeed but it would be without the support of good schools and like-minded peers. In Liverpool, however, not only were there many good schools, but, also, the Pakistani community was very different to that in East Lancashire. There were no textile mills there and the Asians who lived there were predominantly professionals or business people. The chances were that his children, therefore, would have as their friends the children of people who were educated and valued education.

Although his surprising decision proved to be something of a masterstroke, at the time it certainly did not seem that to my sisters and me. Liverpool was an alien world for us. We had become used to a very different kind of life in Brierfield where we had only ever entered people's houses through their back doors. In Liverpool not only did we learn to use the front door but we also had to suffer the indignity of telephoning before we called round. Who on earth did these people think they were? They certainly did not act like those we were familiar with. They seemed to have something of a superiority complex, and, for the first time, we encountered the mutual appreciation society which was the world inhabited exclusively by Asian doctors. I had been brought up to call all adults either uncle or auntie yet here I was faced with children referring to close family friends as Doctor so and so.

It was all bizarre, impersonal and quite off-putting at the time. It was also strange to have no other Pakistani families in our street, or the next, or the one next to that. Nothing seemed within walking distance unlike our former home where taking public transport anywhere was a rare occurrence. As we did not have a car at the time any journey over a mile or two was by bus. Going to the mosque could only be achieved by bus. Going to the city centre was by bus. It was all a bit overwhelming. My school was a good twenty-minute walk away and once there I had to suffer the indignity of fellow pupils laughing at my accent and calling me a "woolly back".

There may initially have been an absence of the comfort that familiarity brought with it in Brierfield but, thankfully, there was also the absence of the negative aspects of life there. Being part of the large Gujjar community had its advantages, especially if your family was well-regarded, but it also carried with it the constant attention of others who were interested in your business. This meant that those who may have had a grievance with a family back in a village in Pakistan, would carry on that grievance with relatives who lived in England. Many a grudge was perpetuated in England, over issues that originated in Pakistan, and often these grudges led to violence, particularly in the case of Gujjars who were not averse to exchanging blows. We children did not see any violence ourselves, but were aware that it was never too far away. On one occasion someone did not take too kindly to my father providing advice to a particular individual, and decided to mark their displeasure by sending a brick through the window one evening. For us this was a rare occurrence, in fact, the only one that I am aware of, but I quite regularly heard stories about others getting into fights. The Gujjar taxi driver/drunken English passenger interface was a common refrain of 1970s Lancashire, and my father appreciated that this environment was to be avoided. Futile clan grudges over village politics and scrapping with drunks was not the life he intended for me and it was not a life led by those we encountered in Liverpool. Strange though these new neighbours appeared, they seemed to get on with their lives without fighting with others, or each other, and seemed more interested in making a success of whatever it was that they did.

Although we are still talking about the late '70s and, therefore, the age of just three television channels (on our black and white telly), no "tinternet", and no obsession with fancy food, pretty soon after our move to Liverpool I did begin to feel that it was clearly a more advanced environment than the one I was accustomed to. It was a city after all, and one which was inhabited by people who were only strange because they were, in fact, quite sophisticated, relatively speaking. They had jobs that did not involve them getting their hands dirty. Rather than constantly talking about what was happening in their village in Pakistan they seemed more interested in discussing important topics. Talk of politics was not village politics, but what was happening in the world. General Zia coming to power in Pakistan, the hanging of his predecessor Zulfikar Ali Bhutto, the Russian invasion of Afghanistan and the now famous resistance of the Mujahideen, all formed the new conversations that I was hearing between my father and his friends. And the common thread that seemed to run through all these conversations was Islam. This, in part, was due to the nature of the subjects. General Zia had made it clear that he wanted a more "Islamic" Pakistan unlike that under his predecessor, even if that meant the imposition of Shariah law, which he subsequently did. The Mujahideen resistance of the Russians by means of "jihad" was again a struggle couched in religious terms (and, in fact, wholly supported by an America whose media never tired of extolling the virtues of jihad, that is, if it was against the Russians). Partly, however, the religious nature of the conversations reflected the people with whom the conversations were conducted.

Recently, when reading Zia Sardar's excellent *"Desperately Seeking Paradise"*, I was astonished to discover that within the first few pages he mentioned a Dr Ahmed Zaman Khan. I knew the man well as he was one of my father's best friends, and one of the first people we met upon moving to Liverpool. I did not appreciate, however, that he would figure in a book by such a well known Muslim writer, especially one whose views are of a more progressive and thoughtful nature, attributes which could not really be used to describe the dear Doctor. That, however, was exactly why he figured in the book. His "brand" of Islam was, and still is, despite some mellowing over the years, one of absolutes, black or white, right or wrong, with little in the way of grey areas, and in the early 1970s when Sardar first met him he was at his peak in terms of fitness, loudness and zeal. It was entirely understandable that he would be used by Sardar as an example of the nature of Muslim practice in Britain in the early days and to what extent, if any, it had developed from that position since.

Dr Ahmed Zaman Khan was, in fact, a dentist, but the title Dr Zaman was how he was, and still is, known, and he was a larger than life character in more ways than one. He was a giant of a man whose main interests were eating, weight training and Islam. When he was a young man in Pakistan he had been something of a boxer and it was only later that he somehow successfully, and to his own surprise, managed to navigate the academic path which led to dentistry. The wonderful dentition with which I have been blessed meant that my experience of Dr Zaman's dentistry skills was happily brief, but not everyone could boast the same painless visit. The fact that he only had one eye, may, arguably, have impacted on his practice, and he himself joked about how his patients would leave his surgery only to go straight next door to the solicitor's in order to seek legal redress for his, admittedly rather haphazard, re-arranging of their teeth.

Dr Zaman certainly had a good sense of humour and without doubt he was an utterly genuine and honest man. He was also one of the most hospitable people we knew, not only insisting that any visitor to his house stay for dinner, but also putting up many a visitor from abroad, for days, if not weeks on end. He would also, at his own expense, take such visitors on tours the length and breadth of Britain. Such generosity also meant that he had many hosts to look after him when he travelled to their countries. All this was just as well because, at times, it appeared as though he was going out of his way to start a fight. He would pointedly ask female Muslim patients why they were not wearing the hijab, making their visits to the dentist even more uncomfortable than usual. He would insist (perhaps forgetting the Quranic injunction that there is no compulsion in matters of faith) that any Muslim visitor to his house would join in when it was prayer time and it was rare that anyone refused the ex-boxer whose generosity was matched in equal measure by his temper. When others, including his closest friends, suggested to him that perhaps his interpretation of Islam was not the only one, he would often get so animated that it appeared that blows would be inevitable. Happily that never occurred, but many a time I recall the frustration of his guests who, try as they might, could not convince him that Islam did not forbid televisions. But his logic was unique and he would happily go from banning televisions to, a few years later, having several in his house. He would insist on the strict segregation of the sexes where there was any Muslim gathering, yet was more than content to go to supermarkets brimming with "infidel" housewives. Not surprisingly he occupied much of the landscape of late '70s Liverpool and played no small part in the discussions involving Islam.

The Muslim community was starting to find its feet in England, and for various reasons, was now beginning to actively consider its faith and the practice thereof. This was certainly more evident in Liverpool than in the towns of Lancashire and it was clear by now, even to

10-year-old me, that Islam was going to play a significant part in my life whether I liked it or not. It was not just Dr Zaman but several other families whose practise of their faith meant no television. That itself was manageable but some of them were so stern and puritanical in their insistence on others joining in at prayer time that it was quite intimidating to visit them and it was many years before I could understand the reasons for their approach, let alone summon up the courage to question the way that they did things. The UK Islamic Mission was behind much of the zeal being displayed, as it was the major Islamic organisation, especially for the educated among the elder generation. It was hard to argue against much of the good work that it did but the problem lay in the all or nothing approach to faith, which many of its members adopted.

More recently, this organisation has been accused of being part of an international Saudi-funded Wahhabi network but the pejorative undertones that this carries today is due to an unduly simplistic view of what it stood for. It is true that they may have had financial support from Saudi Arabia, which understandably meant that their stance would be one with a distinct Saudi flavour, but, more often than not, this simply manifested itself as religious orthodoxy rather than anything more sinister. In other words, there was not any extremism as we know it today, or even a hint of violence, but what it did mean was that there was a puritanical approach when it came to practising the faith, an approach which made little allowance for differences of culture or accommodations with the practical realities of day to day life in a modern society. The necessity for such accommodations was not so clear at the end of the 1970s when the Muslim community was pretty much left to its own devices. It was still a young community in Britain and one whose children were only just beginning to get involved in the education system. It was only later, when these children began to be faced with two parallel lives, their school friends inhabiting one, and their parents, the other, that some of the more educated and thoughtful Muslim parents began to reconsider the way they practised their faith, realising that it may not be the case that the traditions they had inherited from Pakistan, India, Yemen or wherever, would suffice for England.

For my own family this thought process had yet to begin. My father ensured that his children were taught the basics in order to be Muslim, and, for the time being, that was sufficient. Of more importance was the need to ensure that we all received a good education, as it was this which would ensure our "survival" in a modern society. My father played his part admirably in ensuring that his meagre teacher's salary could enable us to live in a decent part of the city surrounded by good schools and good people. He was ably assisted by my mother who, like many other Pakistani mothers at the time, used to do sewing piecework, from home, to supplement the family income. Between them they somehow managed to stretch to moving to a nicer house within a couple of years of our move to Liverpool. We would now have a garden, a garage and for the first time in our lives could escape the back yards and alleys that came with terraced houses.

My father's purchase of a nice semi-detached house clearly illustrated that he had absolutely no intention of keeping himself and his family in working class surroundings, preferring instead the middle class lifestyle that his colleagues enjoyed. We were all sent to a nearby junior school, which served its purpose well (and, in fact, was recently brought back to my attention when I discovered that the former Attorney General Lord Goldsmith had also studied there). It was constantly drummed into us from an early age that we must do well at school and I, being the eldest, the brightest, and the only boy, felt the pressure weighing heavily on me from my junior school days. My real passion still involved cars, but, although I was disappointed that my dad's first car purchase was a sensible Datsun 120Y, rather than something I could boast about at school, I realised that, to my father at least, cars came a distant second to academic achievement. A lot was expected of me and that pressure only intensified when the time came to apply to a secondary school.

CHAPTER 2

Luck or Blessings

In 1980 the Blue Coat was probably the best school in Liverpool, certainly as far as academic results were concerned. Thirty odd years later, not much has changed in that regard. It was a voluntary aided grammar school, which back then was mostly made up of day pupils, with perhaps 10 per cent being boarders. Its academic results were outstanding year in year out, and my father, being a teacher, had understandably decided that this was the school that I should be going to. The only problem was that entrance was limited, requiring a recommendation from the head teacher of my primary school, as well as "passing" an interview at the Blue Coat. I was reasonably bright, however, but it was a less than encouraging start when the exceptionally bright son of some family friends failed to obtain admission.

I managed to secure the recommendation of Mr Matthews, my primary school headmaster, so now it was off to the interview. I knew how much this meant to my parents, as it was the first time anybody in the family was doing anything like this. I was the eldest child not only in our immediate family, but also out of all my cousins, and as we were still relative newcomers to

Liverpool, I had the feeling that it was not only the family's eyes which were on me but also the wider community's. So, off we all nervously went, my parents and I, to the interview one evening, where, amongst other very general things, I was asked what my favourite subject was at school, and which was my least favourite. Although I later enjoyed studying languages, at that particular time I seemed to be having some issues with French and quite cheerily told the interviewers that it was my least favourite subject. When they enquired why that was so, I, just as cheerily, told them that I thought the teacher was not very good. When they asked who the teacher was, I told them without hesitation, not appreciating at the time that she was the mother of two brothers at the Blue Coat. The interviewers smiled and said I should be more careful in what I say. Something of a faux pas then, but given that my French was not that good, I obviously would not have known what that meant. Luckily for me it was not deemed so great an offence that it prevented me from being offered a place there, and in due course, I went in, all smart and scared witless, on my first day. My father was thrilled and proud, and everyone else around me seemed quite impressed too, so things seemed to be coming together after three years in our new surroundings.

My seven years at the Blue Coat were filled with great memories. My academic achievements were modest, I did enough to progress and ultimately secure a place at university, but I met some of the funniest, sharpest guys one could have the good fortune of meeting, and that included the teachers. My personal favourite was my Latin/history/religious studies teacher Phil Watson. Not only was he a great teacher but he had that finest of qualities in that role, namely, the ability to establish a great rapport with his pupils. His lessons were such good fun that to this day I have no clue as to how I managed to get an A grade in my Latin O level. I returned to the school in 2011 to speak at the Founders' Day Service and asked about Mr Watson. I was informed that although he was approaching retirement he was still regarded as something of a legend at the school, but, sadly, although I missed out on meeting him on this occasion, the visit brought back some great memories. One of my memories of him was that he once told us that for years the headmaster had called him Dave and he did not dare correct him. The headmaster was Mr Peter Arnold-Craft, ex-Oxbridge, stern disciplinarian, well capable of putting the fear of God into any teacher, let alone 11-year-old newcomer to the school. Credit to him, however, as he was the head for all the time I was there, and clearly played a large part in maintaining the high academic standards each year.

Another memory of Mr Watson is one that reflects some of the changes society has undergone in the last quarter of a century. In the '80s, when it was still common for pupils to be caned or "slippered", the last thing one expected from one's teachers was much in the way of sensitivity. They were the teachers and, by and large, the pupils knew their place, especially at schools such as the Blue Coat. If you managed to strike up some friendly banter with a teacher then that was just a bonus. I remember in one of his lessons early on in my school life, he made a couple of jokes which involved me and my race or religion. I thought nothing of it and laughed along. This was, after all, one of my favourite teachers. I was nevertheless surprised when at the end of the lesson he called me back and said words to the effect of, "Look, I say such things in jest, but I hate racism and if ever you are offended by my comments you only have to say so and I won't make them any more". I told him it was no problem for me. I am sure that over the years since I left school he will have adapted his rapport with the pupils to take into account the changes in what was expected of people in his position, but to be perfectly honest I think I much prefer his approach to the mealy-mouthed political correctness which prevails now, and which hides all manner of unsavoury views. It's just that those who now hold them realise they cannot freely air them in public (unless, of course, they are part of that breed who feel free to abuse on the internet behind the shields of their pseudonyms), and, the fact that they cannot, simply makes them more entrenched in their views, blaming their victims as if political correctness was something invented by them.

The school was not only an enjoyable time for me but also helped shape my future in ways that I did not fully appreciate at the time. As I was one of only two Muslim pupils in my year, not surprisingly, my friends were all white English lads, but, culturally, although there was still a big gap between my life at home and that at school, I did not feel alienated or marginalised in any way. I seemed to get by adequately enough with one foot in each culture, knowing that I was a Muslim, yet comfortable with my English friends and not feeling left out, despite clearly having to miss out on various "social events" as we grew up. This is something that does trouble many young Muslims and may well impact on my own children's lives in due course, but for me it was never an issue. Growing up, I had no interest in going to parties, pubs or clubs and that, coupled with the knowledge that my parents would not allow it anyway, meant that the boundaries were clearly drawn and there was no chance of them being encroached upon. I had sufficient personality to make friendships and did not feel my life was any the less enjoyable simply because there were certain limitations that those friendships operated under. The '80s progressed enjoyably enough and it looked as though I would succeed in getting the education I required in order to attain my goals.

The goal, which I had announced at the ripe old age of nine, was that I was going to become a barrister. Now that sounds either mightily impressive or annoyingly precocious, depending on your approach to these things but, if truth be told, it was probably neither. My parents, like every other Asian parent on the planet, had told everybody that I was going to become a doctor. To be fair, they did not just go round announcing it to all and sundry, but, if somebody remarked that I was a bright boy and enquired what I wanted to be when I grew up, the answer from my parents was always "doctor". For a short while I was happy to go along with this, until, one day it dawned on me that, as I hated blood and goo, perhaps going in to medicine was not the ideal career choice. I was also smart enough to realise that we had a close family friend who was a barrister, earning good money, and clearly somebody who had my father's respect. So, without knowing exactly what a barrister did, I proclaimed that I wanted to become a barrister. Not only had it got me out of having to become a doctor, but it was also good for my parents who were now well settled in the social life of Liverpool's Pakistani community, and no doubt enjoyed telling their friends about their son's ambition to become a barrister.

One of the places where the community gathered was at the monthly meetings of the Circle of Literary Friends. This was a Pakistani cultural organisation that met regularly and discussed Pakistani history as well as related Islamic topics. The events consisted of some talks, food, and generally getting to meet other members of the not very large community. One of my father's good friends was the founder of this group and we children were roped in to not only attending the meetings, but even speaking at them. Even for a good teenager like me, these meetings were utterly boring. My father, however, saw the bigger picture and used them to develop my public speaking. He would write a speech for me, sometimes in English, sometimes in Urdu (which certainly impressed the other families), and I would practice it at home before dutifully reading it out in front of everyone. In due course I even received a Young Speaker of the Year award for this, presented by David Alton MP (now Lord Alton), but at the time I was rehearsing, I just felt like I was being punished in some way.

It was also an opportunity for my father to put to use the considerable knowledge he had about Pakistani and Muslim history. He was something of an authority on Jinnah, the founder of Pakistan, as well as on Iqbal, the poet and Islamic scholar who was the inspiration behind the movement for Muslim independence. At the time all I did was read out what my father wrote, and very little of the knowledge actually permeated through my skull, but one thing that did stand out was the fact that my father seemed to have the utmost respect for these two individuals. Both of these men had been called to the Bar in England; with Jinnah going on to forge such a successful career in London that he had a chauffeur driven Bentley in the 1930s! Iqbal, however, was more of a thinker, perhaps dreamer, who realised that the ill-treatment of Muslims in India required a separate state by way of solution. He was also by all accounts a wonderful poet who, through his verse lamented the state of Muslims in the world and exhorted them to improve themselves so that they were befitting the vicegerency which had been bestowed upon them by their Creator.

My secondary education, therefore, was all geared towards this one goal, gaining a university place in order to get the law degree I would need in order to become a barrister. As ever in my life, I was incredibly lucky, or as I would say, blessed. I had secured admission to the best school in Liverpool on the back of a recommendation from my headmaster and a mildly amusing interview. I had somehow managed to get 10 O levels, which sounded good even though the grades were hardly spectacular. And now, I had managed to fail one of my A levels and still do enough to get a place at Manchester University, one of the best universities in the country, especially for law, when harder working, brighter pupils had narrowly missed out on their universities of choice. Not for the first time I had landed on my feet and felt very fortunate.

I have no doubt that one of the reasons I did not perform particularly well in my A levels, is because when I was supposed to be revising for them, I decided to do this work in our front lounge. This was also where my father kept all his books, most of which were on the subject of religion. Instead of studying for my A level Economics, which was shockingly dull, I preferred to read his religious books, and it was here that my first genuine religious convictions were formed. Up until then I had been content to believe in Islam because I was taught to, but now my "beliefs" were beginning to develop.

I encountered a world, which suddenly seemed to place me on a much firmer footing. Although I had adjusted well to the fact of occupying two cultures, my religious knowledge was fairly limited and certainly did not fill me with confidence. Also I knew next to nothing about Pakistani history and its personalities. Yet, now, my father's books were not only introducing these topics to me, but were doing so more readily because they seemed to have ignited an interest in me. Now the endless conversations he had with his friends began to make sense to me and I started to appreciate not only their content, but just as importantly, their tone. It was not lost on me that the common themes in these conversations, and in his books, were Islam, education, integrity and responsibility, and how these things did not occur in combination as often as they should. It was also somewhat bizarre, perhaps, that my father had initially intended to go to the Bar like Jinnah and Iqbal, he had a religious outlook that mirrored that of Iqbal, he admired the political acumen and principled tenacity of Jinnah, and his son (whose name translated as Light of Faith) had chosen to be a barrister and was now developing religious views which in time would take on board many of the themes found in his books.

These books, however, reflected a world of Islam, which even I could see was noticeable by its absence. Iqbal was reminding his audience of the past glories of the Muslim world, from Cordoba to Samarkand, but painfully pointing out that what was left behind now was merely a shell, both in terms of the character of the people and the remnants of their faith. He was urging the Muslims of his day to awaken from their slumber but little seemed to have changed in the following hundred years or so. Yes, there was now independence from colonial rule for many Muslims throughout the world, but this in itself, had not necessarily improved their lot, nor had it enhanced the respect of the Muslim world. Jinnah, had undoubtedly succeeded in gaining an independent Muslim state in the shape of Pakistan, but what had that country achieved on the world stage since? It may well have suffered from his untimely death, as well as from being hamstrung by India and Britain at inception, but how many of its faults could it attribute to others? The rampant corruption, dishonesty and lack of human dignity, which even as a teenager I could see, were a world away from the integrity displayed by Jinnah. And to add insult to injury, instead of working to overcome these flaws there were too many Pakistanis who were content to point out that Jinnah was a "bad" Muslim who drank alcohol, which was forbidden in Islam. This was to be my first understanding of the extent to which the form of Islam was beginning to overshadow the substance, but such thoughts were only just being sown.

Distracting though they were, thankfully the books did not prevent me from getting the necessary grades in order to go to university and so, in the summer of 1987, my father had the pre-university "chat" with me. He had never really had to tell me about the do's and don'ts of life, as I had generally been well-behaved. As for the facts of life, well there was no way he was going to explain them in any detail. Now, however, there was a conversation which he felt had to take place, which involved both the facts of life and some do's and don'ts. As ever, it was all conducted in a very British way, with tremendous dignity (aloofness) and respect (shyness), partly because he did not want to say much, and I certainly did not want to hear much. In short, he said a few words about one's "character" and how university was the place where this would be tested. I, with my customary insight, understood this to mean "no hanky-panky with your tickle tackle" and there, matters were left to rest. At that time this approach was not difficult for me as I still saw life in stark terms. Things were black or white, right or wrong, and as long as you followed the rules, then you would be fine.

It follows of course that I did not even set eyes on a woman until I got married some twenty odd years later, but that inherent virtue aside, I was particularly ill-equipped for such endeavours in any event. I had been to an all boys school. I had not had any female friends, let alone any girlfriends, and here I was in a flat in Manchester with seven English lads who were hardly the last word in romantic exertions. A couple of them had girlfriends back home, one had the odd female "acquaintance" but, being from Yorkshire, generally preferred beer to women, and the rest were practically hand-picked by the good Lord Himself (moving as He does in mysterious ways) to help ensure that I was not tempted to stray. What followed, therefore, were three years wasted, I mean spent, on getting a law degree, and not much else. Looking back on my university years, I am pretty sure that if I had befriended some Muslim lads for those three years, the chances of emerging with an unblemished "character" might not have been so great. Certainly, for many of them it was the opportunity they had been waiting for, with no parents, no restrictions, in fact little to stop them enjoying themselves.

Of course there were also other types of Muslim students. I would see them every week in a makeshift prayer room where they would conduct the Friday prayer. They were undoubtedly sincere and devout, but the strange thing was, however, that I was not particularly drawn to them either. I said my prayers with them but although they seemed like decent guys they were hardly the type I wanted to hang out with. There was also an Asian Society, predominantly made up of students of an Indian background (in those days they seemed to show much less pride in being Indian than is evident now and there was no Indian Society), and they were much more fun-loving but, as bhangra gigs were not really my thing either, I did not join their number. Bizarrely I ended up spending most of my time with my flatmates, who were a pretty decent bunch, had no issues with me being Muslim and not joining in their nights out, and were actually good fun. We all got on so well that give or take one or two changes to the group, most of us stayed together for the full three years. I suppose they suited my life in the sense that as I had not grown up with many Muslim friends, to artificially go looking for some now would have seemed strange.

The serious Muslim students seemed a bit too "Muslim" which I was also not used to, so I soon began to attend the local mosque in Manchester for the Friday prayers. This was a typical Pakistani-run mosque where if you had forgotten to wear a cap, some helpful soul would place one on your head for you, oblivious to the fact that this is not, in fact, a religious requirement. The sermons were delivered by an imam who seemed to model himself on the Pharaoh rather than the Prophet, entering the mosque like a king entering his castle, and then proceeding to deliver a sermon of such fiery rhetoric that the simple masses listening were left awestruck, but utterly unenlightened. It was not that he was advocating violence or anything, just that he was all about the style rather than the substance, and rarely, if ever, did you leave the mosque thinking that you had just learned something. In fact, most of the time you did not even know what he had just said. To this day I find it depressing to think of the number of mosques up and down the country, where the opportunity to address, and thereby educate, a captive audience is squandered on a weekly basis.

What made it all the more frustrating was the fact that there we were in the late '80s being thrust onto the front pages over the Satanic Verses affair, and, just when we needed articulate, intelligent leaders to speak up on our behalf, they suddenly appeared conspicuous by their absence. Not only was there little in the way of impressive leadership, but the community had to suffer the further indignity of being lectured to by the likes of Douglas Hurd MP about how it was expected to behave. The same community which by now had been here for over twenty years and had been regarded as hard-working and law-abiding, never rioting and never complaining, was being portrayed as villainous overnight. There may well have been a legitimate debate about the limits of free speech but Muslims were not invited to participate as equals. Rather, they were simply being told what was expected of them. Salman Rushdie was being held aloft by the literary worthies for his amazing insight into the immigrant experience, when such an experience was more accurately, and amusingly, recalled by the average mini-cab driver in Blackburn. People like my father had come to this country and worked day and night to not only improve themselves but also contribute to their new home, while at the same time struggling to hold on to their religious values and identity, and yet it was Rushdie who was the hero. For me this whole episode was bewildering and depressing, but taught me some valuable lessons about leadership, education, and the portrayal of Islam by the western media.

So university for me was not a greatest period in my life and to be fair I should have made more of it than I did, at least on the gaining knowledge front. One feature that was a highlight, however, was my friendship with Andrew Yerrakadu. He was a student from New York whose parents were originally from Guyana and of an Indian background, which meant that he looked as Asian as me. We could have probably passed for brothers, although he was twice the size of me as he was also a talented weightlifter. We got on great and spent most days together. He rarely drank, and as he had a girlfriend back in the USA, he was not one for chasing the ladies either. He was also a practising Christian and would have gone in to the ministry if he had not chosen law, but his explanation of various Christian beliefs was totally new to me. Here was a Christian, who did not believe that "Son of God" was to be understood literally as the physical offspring of the Creator. He had no issues with the theory of evolution, which to me seemed bizarre for a believer, as my own religious outlook was still one of absolutes where there was only room for what I had read in the books, and evolution did not form part of that. Put simply, he was both very religious and very thoughtful, and, for the first time, I had met somebody who seemed to inhabit his religious world very comfortably. Although I may not have realised it at the time, together with my flatmates, Andrew was to influence the way I approached life as a Muslim in Britain, and began to introduce a little more colour into a life which had perhaps been too monotone thus far.

I often describe my university days as a waste. I was not exactly a typical student, or even typical Muslim student; whatever that might be. I did not have the kind of "fun" normally associated with university life, which would not have been so bad if I had emerged with some spectacular academic success but that was never going to happen. Firstly, I was never that bright, and, secondly, I was doing a law degree simply for the fact that I wanted to be a lawyer, not because I had any interest in the law itself. Very soon after I started working I realised that so little of the degree was relevant to what I was doing, that I may as well have done a subject I was interested in, say history or politics, and then crammed some law into a conversion course for a year to get me through to the Bar finals. But, of course, I believe everything happens for a reason, so what may have seemed like a wasted university life, actually brought me into contact with people whose outlook on life influenced me in a positive way. At the time it may have been incredibly frustrating for me to argue with Andrew about say, the Satanic Verses, (Lord knows Andrew loved to argue) but its benefits were only appreciated much later. Andrew and I both graduated and then went to Bar school together before he returned home to sit the New York Bar exams and I began my search for a pupillage.

I had applied to, amongst others, a set of chambers in Liverpool, which had a good reputation for criminal and family work, and it was the former that I was interested in. Their interviewing procedure was that a few of them would come to a London hotel, spend a weekend there interviewing prospective candidates, and, if they were impressed by any, they would invite them to come and spend a day or two in chambers so that others could get to meet them. My interview took place on a Saturday morning. It was my first pupillage interview and it seemed to go well enough. Thankfully they asked no legal questions that I can remember, preferring to concentrate on the more pressing issue of whether I was a red or a blue. Once I had given them the correct answer (LFC of course), the interview proceeded in a relaxed and friendly way and I went back home reasonably pleased. Later that same day they rang asking me to spend the following Tuesday and Wednesday with them in Liverpool. So I went home for a few days, spent a couple of them in chambers and at the end of the second day was told that I had an offer of a pupillage. I duly went back to my course and was asked how the visit went. I nonchalantly announced that I had been offered a pupillage.

That was when I realised the enormity of what had happened. My simple-minded view up until then had been that you got all your pupillage offers and then decided which one to pick. It was only when I began to hear the stories of students decorating their bathrooms with rejection letters that it began to dawn on me how lucky I was. My classmates, who were a tad more realistic than me, could not believe that within four days of my first pupillage interview, I had secured an offer. Once again things had fallen into place for me without much effort or stress on my part. All I had to do was to pass the Bar exams and this I somehow managed the following summer. I could not begin to explain how this happened because 1990–1991 was the first year of the new Bar Vocational course and nobody had a clue what they were doing, tutors included. It all seemed like a lottery but happily for me my number came up and a new chapter of my life was opened.

In the autumn of 1991 I began my pupillage in what was then the Chambers of David Harris QC, or Third Floor Peel House. Robert, my pupil master, was great. To this day he remarks that he only ever asked me to do one piece of work in the whole of my pupillage, and that he is still waiting for it. Well I suppose it was his own fault for being so relaxed about things and preferring to talk about his exotic holidays rather than anything particularly useful to me as a pupil. I do, however, recall one conversation with him that was not so relaxed. At the end of one particular day, when we had returned to chambers from court, he said he needed to speak to me. In fact, he said, "David has asked me to speak to you". I was beside myself thinking what on earth I had done so wrong to prompt my head of chambers to feel the need to speak to my pupil master. I sat down across the room from him. He seemed very nervous which was not like him so I figured things must be bad. He began with, "...well what it is...I am not married...I live with a friend..." The penny dropped for me, (admittedly, somewhat belatedly, seeing as I had been his pupil for a few weeks by now and had not suspected anything), but that did not stop Robert continuing the uncomfortable conversation. Well, at least he tried to continue the conversation until a shelf stacked with heavy law books came crashing to the ground in the middle of our mutual discomfort. I could not help but think, "Well, if that isn't Divine intervention mate, I don't know what is!"

The rest of that decade pretty much involved establishing myself in my career, buying a house in a nice part of town close to my parents, enjoying having money in my pocket and nice cars to drive, with nothing in the way of serious responsibility, at least not outside of work hours. There was undoubtedly a very visible change in the way I was being treated by people and it really did seem to make a difference when they discovered that I was a barrister. My father's friends now had a new level of respect for me and were more inclined to involve me in their conversations, which were still along the same lines as when I was younger, it was just that I understood them more now. Their criticisms of religious leaders were no different but just made more sense to me now and I began to appreciate more of the nuances that they saw in their faith but which had passed me by up until then. The fact that they managed to inject humour even into their religious conversations also played a part in the development of my religious outlook as I began to realise that there was nothing in the Quran forbidding having a laugh.

In fact, there was not as much forbidding in the Quran as many Muslims would have us believe. The fact that many of the religion's followers saw it as one long list of do's and don'ts did not mean that their approach was correct. The more I read the Quran, and other books about Islam, the more I realised that there was more to this faith than rules and regulations. For the time being, however, I did not have to concern myself unduly with such considerations. That was my father's department. He did the reading, thinking and discussing, whilst I was free to concentrate on my career.

All that was to change, however, in 1999. My father had suffered from prostate cancer for several years and, although, his initial treatment appeared to have been successful, by late 1998 the cancer had returned. He retired from teaching in November 1998 and one of the first things he wanted to get sorted was the operation to remove his prostate gland. He was booked in for his operation on the 19th March 1999. We were warned it was a lengthy operation, somewhat complicated by the fact that he had previously undergone radiotherapy. It well enough, though, and after it he was to spend a week or so recuperating in hospital. I took a few days off work and thought I would go and spend time with him although he, himself, did not see the point of me sitting there all day.

On the 23rd March I was planning to go in and see him in the afternoon. I was at home at about 11 o'clock in the morning when my sister rang to say the hospital had called urgently telling us to get to the hospital as my father had collapsed. I made my way from my house while my sister took my mother. We arrived at the hospital at the same time, worried but not for a moment expecting the news we received. We were taken into a separate room to be told that my father had apparently had a heart attack due to a pulmonary embolism, and had passed away. Our world had suddenly fallen apart.

My mother was beside herself. Even to this day she understandably feels bitter that they were unable to enjoy his retirement, but that day in the hospital she felt like she had lost a limb. My father's best friend just happened to arrive at the hospital minutes later and could not believe the news he was hearing. I almost felt more sorry for him than myself, knowing that he and my father, who saw each other almost everyday, had been looking forward to his retirement so that they could spend even more time together. Although my sisters and I were all grown up and involved in our careers by now, it began to dawn on us in the ensuing days just how much we had come to rely on my father, and how much of a void his passing would leave. He was the source of our family's respect, the voice of reason; the man to whom everyone turned for the answer. That was all gone now and we would have to fend for ourselves. We obviously coped, but even now I look back on the three following years as being nothing but a blur, in which I seemed to be operating on some kind of autopilot.

At the time my father's death seemed like a big mistake. It was so unexpected it just did not make sense. He had his retirement to look forward to and so much still to offer, not just to us but to everyone he encountered. I, for one, had much still to learn from him. It took a long time for me to realise that, untimely though it may have been, it was part of a bigger plan.

One particular day, a few months later, I was asked by some of his friends to attend a local inter-faith meeting so that his colleagues there could pass on their condolences to me in person. I did attend, met some wonderful people, appreciated the efforts they were making, and felt that perhaps I should carry on where my father had left off. I began to get involved in inter-faith work and speak about Islam when opportunities presented themselves. Those opportunities in turn blossomed, and I found myself having embarked on the path, which would ultimately lead to this book.

CHAPTER 3

Religion or Science (Or Both)?

I had been brought up as a Muslim and I dutifully obeyed the requirements of my faith as well as my parents. Although they expected certain standards from me it was rarely that they actually articulated any specific demands. This was partly because, when my sisters and I were growing up, much was left unsaid with regard to what we should or should not do. My own mother's recollection from her childhood, that her parents only had to look at her in order for her to check her behaviour, may well be something of an exaggeration, but, speaking as a parent now myself, I can confirm that unquestioning obedience from one's offspring is not as prevalent today as it was when I was younger. My parents simply did not need to spell things out to me, as I knew myself what was expected of me. (Interestingly enough, in time, this approach also informed the way I followed my religion as, in due course, I grew out of being interested in the minutiae of the rules and regulations, preferring instead to find my own way in adhering to the spirit of the faith, rather than getting unduly hung up about the specifics. This, of course, did not mean that my approach was an undisciplined hippy type student quest to pursue some esoteric truth through a cannabis-induced haze, but, rather, that I came to recognise that blindly following the rules was not what Islam was all about).

So although my parents had been relatively liberal in the way they introduced me to Islam, it was, nevertheless, not open for debate that I was going to be a practising Muslim. Even so, no amount of good parental teaching can replace having one's own conviction about something, so although my father's conversations, both with me and with others, were clearly a positive influence on my outlook, they were just a small, albeit welcome, step on my own journey. I was fortunate enough to have access to his books and it was this that helped me to establish a firm foothold in Islam by way of personal conviction rather than solely upbringing. Many of my friends took a different route to confirming their faith. Some were content to do as they were taught by their parents and did not feel the need to explore their beliefs. They dutifully abided by most of the requirements and as long as they were seen to be practising Muslims, all was well. Others were more thoughtful and willing to look a little deeper into their religion. Often they were unable to discuss their thoughts with their families and soon found the company of those with a similar outlook from their own age group. As we shall see later such closed groups came with their own problems. Not all would go on to become the radicalised youngsters we read of in Ed Husain's *"The Islamist"*, but most were certainly not going to think of Islam in a way other than to mutually confirm the unquestionable rightness of all aspects of orthodox faith.

There had been student Islamic societies since the 1970s but they experienced a shot in the arm after 1979.

The fall of the Shah in Iran, and the invasion of Afghanistan by the Russians, put Muslims back into the headlines and this coincided with the second generation of Muslim youngsters now being in full-time education here in the UK. Islamic student societies were good for all concerned. Youngsters could now be outside the confines of their homes legitimately, and parents could rest seemingly reassured, that their children were socialising with other Muslims, thereby protecting them from the ills of western temptations. (This was not necessarily always the case. In the late '80s I remember that there was a Muslim youth camp held in Hull over a period of several days. I had no inclination to go and stay with the "brothers" knowing that for many of them it was just an excuse to get away from strict homes for a few days and let their hair down. The joy that came with being flicked by a wet towel was lost on me, although, of course, it also meant that I did not get to share in the camaraderie, which such japes encouraged. I preferred to give it a miss, therefore, although I did accompany an older, more responsible, friend who was just attending for one particular afternoon.

Anyway, my suspicions proved well founded after the camp dispersed when it was disclosed that three boys from Liverpool had been expelled from the camp late one night. They had apparently been caught going into Hull town centre to meet up with some similarly errant "sisters". Despite their protestations about only being after a pizza, ("pizza what?" they were asked) they were told to leave the camp immediately. Fortunately for them, they had a car. Unfortunately for them, they had fathers who would have beaten them soundly had they returned home in disgrace, so they decided instead to head off to a friend's house, in Kent. The last (disclosable) part of the story was when a policeman knocked on the driver's door window at about four in the morning and woke him to inform him that the hard shoulder on the M6 was not intended for the lads to get their heads down for a while. To this day I hear Muslims from around the country recall the Hull camp circa 1987 and the Liverpool lads who were expelled, and I am proud to inform them that those guys are now three of my closest friends.)

Happily I did not have to rely on such camps, nor indeed on any of my peers, to develop my interest in Islam. I had read enough by the time I went to university to feel confident in my beliefs, and had yet to experience them being challenged in any meaningful way. Inevitably, however, once there, I began to realise how, for some people, especially many who regarded themselves as intelligent and rational, religious people were to be pitied for their affliction, and to be humoured at best. Their belief in a supernatural being they named "God" was comparable to a child's belief in Father Christmas, and did nothing more than reflect a need in primitive minds to attempt to explain away the vagaries of life. With the arrival of scientific progress, religion had surely become superseded and those who clung to it were acting in the face of all reason. This attitude undoubtedly had an effect on me. At times I would be riled by those who regarded religious belief in this way, although the predominant feeling I had, was a desire to somehow learn to counter such accusations. I was "religious" but did not regard myself as inferior to, or any less rational than, the next man. As for the scientific side of things, however, I was hardly well-placed to address such arguments seeing as one of my claims to fame was to emerge from a top school with 10 O levels, none of which was for a science subject.

Despite my lack of interest in, and worthwhile knowledge of, scientific matters, I happened to read a book called *"The Bible, the Quran and Science"* by a French doctor called Maurice Bucaille. It turned out to be one of those life-changing books that one rarely encounters, as it became the first step on a journey for me on which I attempted to reconcile my religious beliefs with science and reason. In essence, Bucaille's conclusion was that there was nothing in the Quran that was contrary to scientific fact. That itself did not particularly surprise me but more impressive than the conclusion itself, was the way in which Bucaille approached his task. He rightly assessed that the Quran made observations on matters ordinarily regarded as belonging to the realm of scientific enquiry, and therefore required to be considered further by anyone examining whether or not what was said therein, was consistent with modern scientific findings. Bucaille, however, determined that in order to consider those verses properly, he had to learn Arabic. He did so, and, after his subsequent investigations into the Quran, concluded that this book simply could not have been composed by a mere mortal. I was staggered, and somewhat ashamed, to learn that this man's spirit of enquiry had led to him learning a language, which was alien to him, just for the purposes of enhancing his knowledge. I, being a practising Muslim, had contented myself then, as now, with relying on translations of my own Holy Book.

Reconciling religion and science was not a straight-forward task for me for various reasons. For a start, I was never particularly academic, developing, rather, a pragmatic approach to learning, which just enabled me to get to the next stage of whatever it was that I was involved in. It also did not help that, at the time, I was not very interested in science. The exercise, therefore, was conducted in fits and starts, and was not given a high priority by me when it came to considering my faith, with the more mundane concerns of Muslims engaging me more. I also found it troubling that many of the accusations levelled at religion did seem to me to have some support. I was painfully aware that most of the Muslims I encountered, particularly the older generation, were not only little versed in matters of science, but were also insistent on retaining views which were irrational and superstitious in the extreme. To me it was not groundbreaking to think that there was a Divine Architect behind the universe. Many people, much cleverer than myself, shared that view, but it did not follow that they accepted as truth every last assertion made in a "religious" text. Yet that is precisely what many religious people I knew actually did. It was as if to them following a religion granted them licence to discard reason completely. They were content to accept unquestioningly the many myths that often accompanied religion, and did not stop to consider the possibility that such myths were simply a way of conveying a particular message to a particular community at a particular time, and did not, in themselves, constitute some kind of eternal truth. Perhaps more importantly from a Muslim point of view, what such people did not do was to heed the Quran and exercise the powers of reason, which their Maker had granted to them, and exhorted them to use.

It is perhaps all the more surprising in such circumstances that religious belief still prevails. Despite the many flaws of its adherents the idea of religion itself has not only not disappeared but, if anything, is actually in the midst of a resurgence. The fact remains that most of humanity, in most of the world, throughout most of history, has held what can only be described as some kind of religious belief. It has encountered formidable adversaries at various stages, not least the onslaught of scientific enquiry in more recent times, but it has not been extinguished. It has had to respond to the attacks, and at times be deeply self-critical but it remains held by some of the most intellectual, "scientific" people around. It has, undoubtedly, evolved but the fact that it differs in some respects to its former incarnations does not, of itself, prove it is untrue.

Similarly, the fact that religion satisfies a human need also does not in any way prove that "God" does not exist, and it is perhaps here that we need to draw the most important distinction. It is surely the existence, or otherwise, of God, that the argument should be about, rather than the disparate and diverse beliefs of those who purport to be his devotees. There are those who suggest that human beings are "hard-wired" to be religious and it may be that there is some truth in this, particularly as many religious people, Muslims included, believe that humans possess something of the Divine Spirit. Whatever we may choose to call this, whether it is the soul, or the conscience, there is something that seems to distinguish us from the rest of the contents of the Universe, despite the fact that at a molecular level we are all the same.

The resurgence of religious belief, however, is not necessarily a good thing or the best argument in its favour. The criticisms levelled against religion still need to be evaluated. It cannot be denied that there have been instances of it operating as an opiate, dulling the senses of the masses and encouraging them to behave in irrational and destructive ways. It has, on occasion, proved an obstacle to freedom and democracy, and has undoubtedly been used as a tool of those in power. Yet these very same criticisms can, and do, apply to other systems of thought and ways of life, whether they involve a deity or not. It is understandable that the likes of Richard Dawkins and Christopher Hitchens should highlight the crimes of those who profess a belief in God, but there are just as many crimes of atheists, which can be weighed in the balance, and it can hardly be regarded as rational to include the former and not the latter. It does not follow as a matter of logic, nor of practice, that discarding God automatically leads to freedom, happiness and an elevation of one's thoughts. The same human flaws, which operate to the detriment of religious people, also exist in those without religious faith and result in similar problems. It should, therefore, be the eradication of those flaws that should be the goal, rather than suggesting that they only exist because of a particular belief system. Hatred, greed, intellectual laziness, envy and mean-spiritedness are not the sole preserve of believers.

Just as it is right to acknowledge that religious belief has acted to the detriment of individuals and societies, it should also be recalled that it has served to uplift and inspire many others. There are those who can only recall the negative impact of Roman Catholic belief, for example, without remembering how much of a positive impact it had on the arts in the western world. How much has religion influenced major thinkers and leaders who have contributed to the world, both in the past and now? Not only has religious belief inspired artists and musicians as individuals, but it has also inspired communities to fight against injustice and oppression. The belief in a cause greater than oneself can lead to difficulties but can also provide the impetus to challenge an oppressive status quo. Islam may be much maligned now, but there was a time when it freed the enslaved, empowered women, gave life to the female infant who was condemned to die, and provided equality and dignity to the downtrodden. The fact that it may not be fulfilling such noble purposes now should give cause for reflection about why not, rather than jettisoning the entire premise of religion. This noble potential of religion is, in my view, one reason why it cannot and will not fade into obscurity, despite the fact that it is a potential, which is not always realised.

To some, the challenges that science poses for religion simply cannot be met. Vague assertions about matters, which cannot be empirically established, are regarded as the high point of religious belief, while in many cases religious beliefs can be positively shown to be false. Evolution is the trump card played by those who wish to "prove" the false nature of religious faith. For example, the "Creation myth" is regarded as simply that, a myth, which holds that the universe was created in six days, rather than the billions of years we now know to be scientific fact. Two random people called Adam and Eve were not mysteriously dropped onto the planet to propagate and set forth the chain of events that led to us. Accordingly, there is no paradise of milk/honey/virgins waiting for us if we believe in the right god, or a hell of fire, eternal damnation and, presumably, girls who are not virgins, if we do not. And now, in our modern age, humanity has advanced to the extent that it has learned that all events have a rational, scientific explanation and that the idea of an "act of God" had merely been an explanation for the primitive, unsophisticated mind, with its only remaining function being to help insurance companies avoid paying out on their policies. Yet, not only does such an analysis take for granted that religious texts suggesting the above can only be understood literally, but it is also based on the premise that there are a finite number of questions to be asked about all that is in existence, and that scientific enquiry provides all the answers to these questions. We shall return later to the question of understanding religious texts literally, but for now it is the question of science being able to provide all the answers that concerns us.

Now I have considered all this scientific stuff (albeit in an analysis which makes beginner's guides appear encyclopaedic) and come to this conclusion. After our centuries of scientific enquiry, our billions of pounds/dollars spent on research and space travel, our dismissal of religious myths as well as others, we are still not even close to knowing the extent of what is "out there". That may be understandable given the size of the universe. Perhaps more perplexing, however, is that we still do not have definitive answers for even the smallest units of matter. There are those who will not be moved from the conclusion that none of this proves the existence of God, and of course, it does not, at least not in any empirical way. There is, however, the opposing view held by others, who conclude that not only does such scientific enquiry leave open the *possibility* of there being a God, but over and above that, the more one explores science, the more the idea of God as the answer becomes the only *rational* explanation. There are intellectual heavy-weights who occupy both camps so how does the layperson resolve the issue? Does it ultimately come down to a matter of faith? Faith in science or faith in religion? Are the two incompatible? When we talk about faith are we talking about blind faith or is there such a thing as a rational or reasonable faith based upon evidence?

For me, it was the sheer numbers, which helped sway the argument. If we take as our definition of rational; "that which is consistent with or based upon reason" then we understand that what we are talking about is exercising one's mind rather than one's emotions. (Let us leave to one side, for now, the fact that we only use a tiny fraction of the potential of our brains at any given time. It remains a mystery, therefore, as to what amazing feats we could achieve if we tapped into our full potential. We are certainly aware of examples of people who might suffer from conditions such autism, who have phenomenal mathematical capabilities despite not having had any formal training in that field, but there is also the suggestion that tapping into the reserves of the brain's immense power could free up other hidden talents such as telepathy and extra-sensory perception. Whether there is anything in such suggestions is beyond the remit of this discussion but, if so, it could certainly have implications for the whole idea of religion.) When exercising our powers of reason, however, we find that there can come a point at which a proposition that began as reasonable, becomes unreasonable. As a matter of pure logic something may well be *theoretically* possible, but it is so improbable that, at least for the purpose of any meaningful consideration by our minds, it is not *practically* possible.

The scale of what is "out there" matters to me for two reasons. Firstly, as stated above, it has implications for my analysis of what is reasonable or rational. If, for example, the numbers are beyond comprehension then what effect does this have on my acceptance that something happened just by chance? As we noted earlier, my lack of scientific background may well explain my readiness to be amazed by the numbers I encountered, but this only provides a partial explanation. The facts are staggering for anyone.

I have to admit that it was a complete shock for me to discover that the solar system I had learned about at school, was not the simple straightforward picture that I had in my mind, a picture which had the sun at one side of the page, with Pluto occupying the furthest point across from it, and our planet Earth occupying a convenient spot in between the two. I struggled to get my head around even the initial facts I was discovering. For example, that the solar system which I attempted to picture in my mind, was, in reality, one in which all the planets, moons, asteroids and other bits and pieces, occupied less than one trillionth of the available space! Right, so that at least established that the solar system was pretty big. It made sense, therefore, that the pictures I had seen of it had to show everything close together just to make it visible on a single page. However, it was not just that there was a lot of space *between* the planets but that there was a lot of space in the solar system *beyond* the planets. So Pluto, rather than marking the end of the solar system, was, in fact, only one fifty-thousandth of the way to the edge of it. The crazy numbers were now beginning to multiply.

That solar system, however, huge though it was, did not signify all that was out there. Rather, it was just one member of a vast galaxy, the Milky Way, containing perhaps 200 to 400 *billion* stars, of which the sun was just one. This galaxy was roughly 100,000 light years in diameter,(a light year being 5,878,000,000,000 miles) so, even if we were able to travel across it at the speed of light, it would take us hundreds of generations to cross it. So, having established that the Milky Way is unimaginably huge, I next learned that it is, in fact, only one galaxy and, although there is no certainty about how many galaxies there are in the universe, estimates range from 100 to 200 billion, (although some estimate up to 500 billion), with each one containing billions of stars. One estimate, therefore, of the number of probable planets in the universe is ten billion trillion! At least that has cleared that up then. If only. It may help us in beginning to appreciate the extent of the universe (about a million million million million or 1,000,000, 000,000,000,000,000,000 miles across), but that is only the visible universe. There are theories, however, that the universe at large, or meta-universe is much larger still, and that the number of light years to the edge of this unseen universe would be written not "with ten zeroes, not even a hundred, but with millions".

That brings me to the second reason why the scale of all that is out there was important to me. It gave some perspective, however surreal, to my presuming to question why, if there was a Creator, I could not perceive him. "I" could not even be described as a speck on a dot on a speck on a dot, so how was I qualified to question the existence of the Creator of all that existed out there, particularly as I had not even learned to use anywhere near the full potential of my brain? It must be said that just because the universe or even meta-universe is so vast, it does not necessarily follow logically that there has to be a creator of it all. It may just be that it is part of human nature to be overly impressed by sheer magnitude, and, just because the universe is bigger than we can possibly imagine, it does not mean there has to be a role for an architect-in-chief, or Divine instigator of all that flowed from the Big Bang, including human life.

After all, the very size of the universe meant that, "if there are many universes, each governed by a differing set of numbers, there will be one where there is a particular set of numbers suitable to life. We are in that one". So the sheer scale of it all means that there is bound to be some place where life could form, and, happily for us, we happen to be on it. For my understanding, however, this was an insufficient explanation. Firstly, because it relied upon random chance, and secondly, because it was not just the big numbers that impressed me. As a matter of common sense, the human mind was bound to struggle to comprehend the extent of the universe given its size. What was a surprise, however, was the fact that human intellect also seemed to struggle with even the smallest units of existence.

On my scientific quest I discovered that living organisms are made up of cells, which in turn are made up of billions of molecules of many hundreds of different types. The average human cell is 20 microns wide, or about two-hundredths of a millimetre and it is in this tiny area that we find the variety of molecules, such as the billion ATP molecules, and the minimum of 100 million protein molecules. This, of course, is not as small as it gets. Molecules consist of at least two atoms, each one being one ten-millionth of a millimetre! Small enough? Unfortunately not. It was sufficient in the 19th century to explain that matter consisted of atoms but within a hundred years it was discovered that atoms themselves had their constituent parts: protons, which have a positive electrical charge, electrons, which have a negative electrical charge, and neutrons which have no charge. Neutrons and protons make up the atom's nucleus, itself one-millionth of a billionth of the full volume of the atom, but containing almost all the atom's mass. Unsurprisingly perhaps, we still have not reached the smallest unit within the constituents of an atom. Quarks and gluons form protons and neutrons while neutrinos possess one ten millionth of the mass of an electron!

The facts about the size and constituent parts of the atom are perplexing enough on their own, without us even considering the behaviour of those constituent parts. Yet when we venture to attempt just that we discover a sub-atomic world where electrons can jump from one orbit to another without travelling across any intervening space, a world of quantum physics which requires two bodies of laws, quantum and gravitational, in an effort to explain it. In an attempt to draw the two together the superstring theory (and its eleven dimensions) was formulated! So much for my ten O levels.

We have seen how the world of big numbers is perplexing; yet further consideration shows how the micro-world is no easier to fathom. Some of the numbers we have encountered thus far are so huge (estimates of between 100 billion and 200 billion galaxies for example, or the 23 trillion molecules in a human cell), that it is easy to think that all this science is very imprecise. Yet there are other numbers, which suggest that it is anything but. One example is the precise calculation of the way in which hydrogen transforms into helium by converting seven one thousandths of its mass to energy. If that value is lowered slightly, say from 0.07% to 0.06% then the transformation could not take place and the universe would consist of hydrogen and nothing else. Similarly if the value were raised to 0.08% the universe that we need for our survival simply would not exist. What is it that is maintaining this very fine balance? Is it just by pure chance that the whole enterprise is kept afloat?

The possibility of chance playing any significant role in the origin of life is perhaps most vividly illustrated when we look at the formation of proteins by the assembling of amino acids in a particular order. In order, for example, to make collagen (a common type of protein) 1,055 amino acids need to be assembled in exactly the right sequence...spontaneously and by themselves! (Even for a less complex protein, its production by random events is practically impossible, never mind for the hundreds of thousands of types of protein which we actually rely upon.) And having assembled the amino acids in the right sequence, the protein must then fold itself into a very specific shape. How was it that such ordered, yet complex, self-assembly could take place? And having achieved that, the protein would need to reproduce which it cannot do without DNA, which begs the question how proteins and DNA first came into existence?

There have been famous experiments, such as that by Stanley Miller in 1953, attempting to synthesize life, but not only have they been unsuccessful (save for some "inorganic" molecules), they have been unsuccessful in controlled conditions. When life was first formed on Earth, the conditions were not those of test tubes in laboratories. There would have been a myriad of hostile environmental forces that the initial cell would have had to contend with. Assuming for a moment, therefore, that life did spontaneously spark into existence, having achieved that improbable success, rather than just be destroyed by the next gust of wind, crack of lightning or drop of rain, it would have had to replicate that initial "coincidence" many times over, in adverse conditions, in order to even begin to achieve the kind of complexity that could precede life as we know it. Could this really be achieved by chance or was there a master programmer involved? Which of the two explanations is the reasonable one? When we consider, for example, the simple amoeba consisting of one cell, but carrying 400 million bits of information in its DNA, the idea of a master programmer does not seem so far-fetched.

It is perhaps in the genetic field that the notion of a programmer is most apt. Living cells appear to consist of a veritable Aladdin's cave of information. Inside the nucleus of the human cell are the chromosomes that contain all the information and instructions which are required to create and maintain us. They are made up of DNA, almost two metres of it in each microscopic cell, and possibly as much as 20 billion kilometres of it inside our bodies, with each piece of DNA containing some 3.2 billion letters of coding. The result of all this is that it is enough to provide an inordinate number of unique possible combinations that make us what we are. One figure suggested for this number of combinations is a one, followed by more than three billion zeroes! Did all this information come into our cells just by chance or was it specifically programmed into them by an outside force, or God? The idea of it happening by chance is all the more unfeasible to me when I am reminded that "All the tiny, deft chemical processes that animate cells – the co-operative efforts of nucleotides, the transcription of DNA into RNA – evolved just once and have stayed pretty well fixed ever since, across the whole of nature." This, no doubt, partly explains why scientists themselves still use phrases such as the "mystery of life" or "miracle of life", because the more we think we are approaching certainty and finality in our findings, the more questions we seem to unearth.

Perhaps it was best put by Bill Bryson when he said "The upshot of all this is that we live in a universe whose age we can't quite compute, surrounded by stars whose distance from us and each other we don't altogether know, filled with matter we can't identify, operating in conformance with physical laws whose properties we don't truly understand".

At this point it is perhaps worth pausing to ask ourselves what exactly we mean by proof. As a barrister, there are often occasions, when prosecuting, that scientific evidence has to be presented to a jury. This can relate to, for example, fingerprint or DNA evidence said to link the defendant to the particular crime. Often when presenting such evidence the scientific expert in question asserts that the chances of the fingerprint belonging to anyone other than the defendant are, for example, in the order of 1 in 50 million. Such a statistical probability essentially means, so the prosecution would say, that as far as the jury is concerned, there is proof *beyond a reasonable doubt* that the defendant is guilty.

Given some of the statistical probability I was encountering in the precise realm of science, what conclusions would it be reasonable or rational for me to draw? It is considered entirely reasonable to decide the fate of a man on the basis of the above statistical probability figures. Yet when we see the statistical probability that various components in the universe came about by chance (let alone the probability of the entirety of the components coming together to make the whole enterprise work), we seem to readily accept random chance as the explanation. Is it the reasonable, rational belief, in such circumstances to believe in a Divine creator who is beyond the limited comprehension of human beings, or can it properly be concluded that such figures show that random chance is behind the origins and workings of the universe?

So where does this all leave us? The above meander through some fascinating scientific facts should not be seen as an attempt to trivialise the importance of scientific inquiry. The fact remains that our powers of reason are our best hope in navigating our way through life, at least with some measure of understanding. However, understanding the world around us does not necessarily provide all the meaning we need in order to live out our full potential. We can figure out how the world works, and with this knowledge attempt to harness the forces of nature so we can exploit them and master the physical world. We need to remember two things though.

Firstly, there is more to life than the physical world when we consider that we are composed of the same molecules as all the inanimate things around us, yet we clearly possess a consciousness which science has thus far been unable to explain. (At this point an interesting discussion could be justified about the question of what exactly reality is. Is it just the material? Or, given that our understanding of matter is always based upon our sense perception, and therefore, not ascertainable objectively, could it all just be a dream? Perhaps, however, that is a digression too far, for now.)

Secondly, even the exercise of harnessing nature cannot be done in the absence of a system of values. It is a fallacy to think that science is not concerned with values. Scientific endeavour does not operate in a vacuum. It is worth considering, for example, that the vast majority of research and development expenditure in science goes on military programmes. Clearly this is the result of decisions taken in certain quarters and these decisions invariably involve value judgements. It is as a result of such value judgements that decisions are made to fund the development of ever more sophisticated weaponry, rather than put that money towards finding a cure for cancer. The pure exercise of reason does not necessarily assist us in making the right decisions and may, in fact, serve to lead us further down a destructive path, whether that means destructive to our environment or to our humanity. The values upon which we act, therefore, are to be found elsewhere than in science books.

For Muslims these values and principles are found primarily in their holy book, the Quran. Not only does it purport to contain the guidance that humanity requires to live a life that enriches both materially and spiritually, but for me, it also provides the "evidence" which enables me to move beyond a passive agnostic belief to an active belief in the existence of God. It is a book that exhorts the reader to investigate the natural world, as this is a path that will lead him to a reasoned belief rather than a reliance upon blind faith. It is a book that time and again addresses itself to people "of understanding". Nowhere does it hand over authority to a class of so-called "religious scholars" or "mullahs", in order to lord it over the masses. On the contrary the word *ulema* (plural of *alim*, meaning scholar), when used in the Quran, is used in the context of those who are urged to ponder the rain cycle, animal life, plant life and other aspects of nature. In other words it refers to zoologists, botanists, meteorologists, in short it refers to scientists.

When one looks at the golden age of Muslim civilisation and the numerous intellectual and artistic achievements that it boasted, those who were great mathematicians, physicians, poets and artists, were also religious scholars. Knowledge was not defined narrowly to mean just religious knowledge but, rather, it reflected the true spirit of enquiry encouraged by the Quran. It is a sad indictment of the state of many contemporary Muslim societies that the word ulema is understood to simply mean the bearded guys, armed with a smattering of religious rulings, who are entitled to make pronouncements about how the faithful should live their lives.

The Quran urges humanity to fulfil its potential by understanding the world around it. It illustrates that the achievements of Muslims scientists in the golden age – which we shall look it in greater detail in due course – were not despite the Quran, but *because* of it.

However, not only did it contain the inspiration for, and commanding of, scientific enquiry but it also contained scientific references which could not have been authored by a human being in 7th century Arabia. The findings of Maurice Bucaille, and others, showed that the claim of the Quran that it was not a human product but a divine work which was nothing short of a miracle, seemed to me to have some force. After all, the only possible author of this book would have been the Prophet Muhammad, yet there is no suggestion that he ever authored any other document, let alone such a world changing mixture of prose and poetry. I recalled a Christian Arab friend of mine from my university days who told me that he read the Quran, not because he believed it, but because the Arabic was so perfect. This was a grand work of literature as much as anything else. The Holy Prophet was no literary great; on the contrary according to Muslim history he was illiterate. Yet here was a book the recitation of which reduced men to tears.

It was also a book containing scientific material which the Prophet would simply have been unaware of; the reference to two bodies of water (fresh and sea water) which did not mix; the description of the sun and moon using two different Arabic words for "light", one of which denoted something which generated its own light, while the other referred to something with reflected light; the verses pertaining to embryology referring to the foetus as something which "clings", it only being discovered centuries later that the foetus does, indeed, cling to the uterus wall. These and other examples were sufficient to convince me that this was not a book authored by a human being.

And, perhaps its greatest achievement was its assertion that this time it would be God Himself who would safeguard the book. Earlier scriptures may well have been revised and altered but this was a message for eternity and would be protected. I could not understand how this promise had been kept and that there were no subsequent "editions" of the Quran unless it truly was safeguarded. I had not even done a fraction of the research into the Quran that true scholars such as Bucaille could claim, but the little I had done was more than enough to convince me that here was the evidence that supported the idea of the existence of God.

Ultimately, for me therefore, my limited scientific enquiry does not move me further away from a belief in God, but, on the contrary, reinforces my understanding that there must be an intelligent force behind the entirety of what is out there. It helps me make sense of what is around me, and, in developing even a rudimentary understanding of the complexity of life, I can begin to appreciate the wonders of the universe, and consider for myself which conclusions it is reasonable to draw from the available evidence. Science helped to rationalise my religious beliefs so that I did not satisfy myself with childish ideas of an old man with a white beard watching everything from the sky above, whilst at the same time appreciating that the creator of all that exists would inevitably be beyond human comprehension.

It also helped me begin to discard mythology which may have served a particular purpose at a particular time, and focus instead on the values and principles underlying that mythology, and which should underpin the way I live my life. Science reinforces the Islamic view that there is an underlying unity in life so that we do not compartmentalise the spiritual and material aspects but, rather, strive to understand the totality of our environment thereby moving closer to our creator. Only then are we best placed to benefit from the guidance available to us and which we need in order to fulfil our potential and live a life befitting human beings, rather than other sentient creatures inhabiting the planet.

CHAPTER 4

Have Muslims
Always Been "Thick"?

For centuries Western civilization has prevailed. There may well be a degree of consternation in certain quarters that the future is going to be one in which the East exerts its not inconsiderable might, particularly given the apparently unlimited ambition and economic growth of the likes of China and India, but, the fact remains, that for the time being at least, it is still the West which is regarded as being the rightful home to the leadership of the world. Such is the degree to which this belief has become ingrained that, in the West at least, we even regard our current economic plight as a temporary aberration, rather than being possibly symptomatic of any underlying structural or ideological weakness. (Whether our views on the economic situation are accurate or not only time will tell, and we shall consider this further later in this book.) For our present purposes the argument, quite understandably, is that the West has every right to feel pre-eminent, given its record of success, particularly in the field of scientific achievements and consequential material development.

There is no doubting the great forward leaps which were made in the West, particularly in the last six centuries, but one also has to bear in mind the provenance of a history that has largely been written by the victors. We all read Shakespeare at school, as any student of English should, but we would struggle to name any poets from other countries, perhaps making our belief that he was the greatest poet who ever lived, less than robust. Similarly, our understanding of the rest of the world's contribution in fields other than literature also has its limitations. It can be argued perhaps that an Anglophile or Eurocentric approach to such issues can hardly be criticised given where we are living, but, in the age of the global village, an insight into the thinking of others would not go amiss. Nowadays it makes obvious sense for business reasons to have some respect for the sensibilities of the Chinese, and we are very familiar with this approach, particularly as a similar outlook has informed the way we have dealt with oil rich Arab regimes in the past. Such "respect", however, is far removed from genuine understanding, and it is the latter that brings communities together, rather than the tolerance of merely putting up with each other.

We hear of our broken societies, yet continue to ignore possible avenues of mutual understanding that could act as the mortar missing between our communities. At a time when the traditional areas where communities could intermingle are becoming scarcer by the day, with many of the old workplaces such as factories and mills having disappeared, and even the nature of the high street altering considerably, with the increase in online shopping and out of town retail parks, extra thought needs to be given to what can bring people together. Otherwise the alternative is a path that will increasingly diverge until it becomes too late to refer to what is left as society. This is already happening in many English towns, particularly, and sadly, ones with large Muslim communities, and needs to be addressed sooner rather than later if the social cracks are not to widen. Muslims, themselves, need to wake up and ask whether they are contributing to increased understanding or increased mistrust.

Areas for mutual co-operation need to be identified as a matter of urgency. In some cases this can happen organically, such as practical projects that bring neighbourhoods together. Despite media coverage, which suggests that Jews and Muslims are forever foresworn to despise each other, schools such as the King David Schools in Liverpool and Birmingham are perfect examples of Muslims actively seeking education for their children in Jewish schools because their priority is education. The schools in turn are happy to take the pupils. Both communities benefit and it is another small step towards each other rather than in opposite directions. In 2012 at least one happy Jewish-Muslim story did find its way to the BBC website and involved a synagogue in the USA opening its doors to the local Muslim community who needed some extra prayer space for the festival of Eid. Our shared humanity demands such mutual effort but we need not wait for practical needs to arise. There is a long history of mutual intellectual co-operation, which needs to be revived and topics for discussion resuscitated.

One particularly neglected area of potential understanding is that of Muslim scientific achievements. Not only did they have a significant impact on the understanding of science in the west, but they also often took place in Europe itself, so were European achievements just as much as specifically Islamic ones. My own education, as highlighted previously, consisted of seven productive and enjoyable years at the best school in Liverpool. One of my favourite subjects was history, which I studied through to A level. Yet, despite this, I do not recall at any stage studying the history of Cordoba in Spain. Here was a city which, a thousand years ago, was described as the "ornament of the world", boasted facilities that the rest of Europe could only dream of and achieved all this through the mutual endeavour and co-operation of the three monotheistic faith communities, yet this story was deemed unworthy of telling to contemporary generations.

A couple of decades or so later, I may have left school long behind but perhaps the issues are even more important, given that others are still questioning whether or not Muslims can play a useful part in Europe, or, for that matter, the west generally. One might have thought that reminding ourselves of a time when they not only contributed, but, led the way, in many fields, would form a vital part of our education but it seems not. Perhaps those young Muslims who are often described as marginalised and, therefore, vulnerable to radicalisation would feel so much less alienated if they could be taught of the contributions of their ancestors. At the same time those non-Muslims brought up on a diet of anti-Islamic news may feel differently about their Muslim neighbours if they could see a side of them kept well hidden for so long. Yet rather than this seemingly obvious approach to educating our youth, we prefer instead to continue to peddle stories which reinforce stereotypes of western superiority, and, thereby continue to bolster assumptions about the inferiority of the Muslims, whilst at the same time remind young Muslims that they really are alien to, and therefore have little stake in, this advanced society.

One popular myth that continues to hold the imagination of millions, is that of the Renaissance and the preceding Dark Ages. The received history is that the Renaissance emanated from Italy in about the 14thcentury and had its origins in ideas from Florence in the late 13th century. The widely held belief remains that it was essentially a European Christian phenomenon and, of course, Renaissance literally means "rebirth", further reinforcing the impression that it arose almost out of nothing, with Christian European minds simply being awakened from their slumber. Although those responsible were Christians, the origins of the Renaissance could really be attributed to more secular minded humanists such as Dante. The humanist movement was given further impetus by the influx of eastern scholars after the fall of Constantinople in the 15th century, bringing with them important books and manuscripts as well as the achievements of Greek scholarship. It was now Europe's good fortune that the curtain could finally come down on an era characterized by religion and superstition. Although this view of the Dark Ages is now criticised in some circles, the fact is that it was certainly being taught regularly not so long ago.

In this chapter we shall be considering primarily what had been going on in the Muslim world by this stage, and what impact, if any, this may have had on the Renaissance. Was the Renaissance a "rebirth" out of nothing, or was it essentially a process which was initiated by, and able to tap into, a tradition of rational thought and learning which had already existed for hundreds of years, albeit not perhaps in Christian Europe. As we shall see, the Muslim world from the 8th to the 15th centuries had some outstanding success stories, and, not for nothing, were the 12th and 13th centuries regarded as Islam's "golden age". The spread of Islam, after the death of the Prophet in the 7th century, brought Muslims into contact with other civilisations and cultures, and, therefore, the achievements of those cultures. Rather than ignore these, the Muslims voraciously devoured the expertise and learning that they were encountering, spurred on by their Holy Book, which was exhorting them to seek knowledge as a religious duty. For example, encounters with India brought Muslims into contact with, amongst other things, Indian numerals, and this knowledge they took on board and developed further, leading to the system of Arabic numerals that came to be used in the west.

What happened, therefore, in the Islamic world was that Muslims from the Arabian peninsula were now coming into contact with not only contemporary knowledge from other civilisations, but also their store of the ancient knowledge of the Greeks. Again, their Islamic faith did not prevent Muslims from absorbing all that these "pagan" texts had to offer by way of knowledge, and using it as a basis for further study and development, a far cry perhaps from the modern day attitude towards knowledge in some parts of the Muslim world. It is no secret that Greek learning came to the West as a result of the translations of the Arabs. (Often, in fact, Jewish scholars were involved in the process as they were able to translate Arabic translations of Greek texts into Hebrew, thereby enabling later Latin scholars to translate into Latin from the Hebrew.) Similarly, papermaking came to Europe from China, again as a result of the Islamic expansion eastwards and the underlying theme in these interactions was not just a willingness on the part of the Muslims to receive this body of knowledge, but also to develop it further and improve it where possible. There are those who have erroneously reduced the role of the Arabs to nothing more than translators but even a cursory glance at some of the achievements we shall go on to consider, reveals this to be a patently false assertion.

The Muslims used the classical texts as starting points and were able to improve upon them as a result of the patronage of many generous Caliphs. One has to recall that, at the time, Muslims countries could boast wealth as well as military power and, as is often the case when such attributes exist in empires, it enabled them to attract and fund the scholars carrying out such work. It should also be remembered that such funding was not provided on an informal ad hoc basis but constituted part of wider educational initiatives that included the establishing of universities, libraries and observatories, and it was the abundance of such facilities that attracted scholars from around the Muslim world. The first university, in fact, was established in Cairo while Baghdad was similarly pioneering with hospitals. (It is interesting to note how even the location of the main Baghdad hospital was as a result of some scientific experimentation, with pieces of meat being hung at various locations around the city and their rate of putrefaction monitored, before deciding where best to locate the hospital.)

The Bayt al Hikmah (House of Wisdom) in Baghdad and the libraries of Cordoba and Damascus, contained thousands of manuscripts available to the public at a time when the cities of Europe could only muster a few hundred in the best of their private collections. One of the most impressive European libraries was that at the monastery of St Gall, yet its few volumes pale into insignificance when one considers that even the 13th-century observatory at Maragheh in Iran, had up to 40,000 volumes.

Undoubtedly there was a thirst for knowledge in the Muslim world of the Middle Ages and it manifested itself in a culture of scientific and technological achievement. There is much to lament in the Muslim world today, but it is not just for reasons of nostalgia that we should recall the achievements of the Golden Age. They were real successes, which not only led to Muslims being pre-eminent for centuries in the field of science, but they also arguably laid the foundations of the later successes of Europe and Western civilization. Simply compiling a list of noteworthy Muslim scientists, scholars and thinkers from that period of history, however, would not only be too long and laborious a task, but would also not convey the effect intended here.

Perhaps a more useful approach is to take a few areas, by no means exhaustive, and see what Muslims achieved in each of those areas, with some concluding analysis about any legacy they may have left. Muslim thinkers were by no means restricted to particular disciplines but there were several areas upon which they did seem to focus. Some of their choices were no doubt inspired by their holy book, the Quran, which, in particular, exhorted them to examine the natural world around them as this exercise itself would bring them to a better understanding of God. For present purposes, therefore, the subjects we shall take a closer look at are mathematics, astronomy, chemistry and medicine.

Mathematics formed the basis for much of the achievements of the period we are considering and, once again, studies in this area were precipitated by the Quran, which, for example, laid out complex rules relating to inheritance, which required putting into practice. One of the earliest civilisations with which Islam came into contact was the Persian Empire, and it was largely from there that the Muslims absorbed much knowledge about mathematics, which the Persians in turn had obtained from the Indians. The Arabs, in fact, referred to this system as that of Indian numerals, with the phrase Arabic numerals merely reflecting the fact that Europe learned of it through the Arabs. For the Arabs, however, this was not simply a system to learn, imitate and benefit from. It was something that they applied their minds to, and through various scholars, were able to develop it with their own original thinking.

We find, therefore, that although the numbers one through to nine evolved from Hindu-Buddhist works, it was the Arab scholars who developed this system further with the introduction of decimal fractions by Sind ibn Ali in the 9th century. (In fact although the concept of the zero pre-dated the Muslims, the word itself is derived from the Arabic *sifr*, which became *zefiro* in Italian, later shortened to zero.) The 9th century saw an amazing array of Muslim mathematical talent. As well as Sind ibn Ali there was his colleague al-Khwarizmi and also al-Kindi, the latter perhaps being difficult to label simply as a mathematician given his other talents in the fields of philosophy, optics, medicine, chemistry and musical theory. It was his *On The Use of The Indian Numerals,* however, which played a significant part in the intro-duction of Arabic-Indian numerals to Europe.

Despite there being many renowned Muslim mathematicians, the greatest of all was undoubtedly Muhammad ibn Musa al-Khwarizimi, or **al-Khwarizmi** for short, who lived from 780–840 CE. He was Persian by birth, and took up a place in Baghdad's House of Wisdom. Like so many Muslim scholars of that era, his expertise spanned several disciplines yet, despite his works in the fields of astronomy and geography, posterity rightly records him first and foremost as a mathematician. Today, few might appreciate that the word algorithm is derived from his name, but his contribution to the language of mathematics did not end there. One of his major works was entitled *al-Kitab al-mukhtaasar fi hisab al-jabr wa'l muqabala ("The Compendious Book on Calculation by Completion and Balancing"),* and it is from this that we get the word "algebra". This was the first systematic solution of linear and quadratic equations in Arabic and was based on intuitive geometric arguments using just words rather than the more abstract notation of symbols with which we are now familiar.

Al-Khwarizmi's work on algebra was revolutionary in mathematics but he was also responsible for other significant developments in the subject. It was his *Kitāb al-Jam'wa-l-tafrīq bi-ḥisāb al-Hind ("The Book of Addition and Subtraction According to the Hindu Calculation),* which was translated into Latin and helped to introduce to Europe the system of Arabic numerals which was based on the earlier work done by the Indians. One criticism of the legacy of the Indians was that there was little by way of commentary included in their works. The Arabs, on the other hand, had no qualms about commenting on and explaining fully that which they were setting out, and Al-Khwarizmi went to great lengths in his exposition of the Indian techniques as well as his explanations of the zero. He is further said to have calculated the value of pi to 14 decimal places as well as calculating the circumference of the earth.

Yet like so many of the Muslim scholars of the Middle Ages, al-Khwarizmi's success was not limited to one field. In geography he was able to correct the ancient texts of Ptolemy in relation to the length of the Mediterranean. In astronomy his "zij", or astronomical tables, marked a departure in the Islamic world from merely translating to introducing original thought. These tables included new ways to track the movements of the sun, moon, and five known planets at that time. They were translated into Latin by Adelard of Bath and formed the basis of all future planetary tables. Al Khwarizmi also developed a sundial that could be used at any latitude to tell the correct time. Many mosques eventually installed his sundial, to help with calculating correct times of prayer. He also seems to have developed several versions of the quadrant, a competitor of the astrolabe. Both were analogue computers that used sky positions to tell time and location. And he achieved all this in the ninth century.

The same century also saw another Muslim astronomer and mathematician, Muhammad ibn Jabir al-Harrani **al-Battani** (858 – 929 CE), or Albategnius in Latin, who carried on where al-Khwarizmi left off. Perhaps the greatest difficulty with al-Battani is deciding whether to put him with the mathematicians or the astronomers, such was the significance of his work in both fields. Although he was an astronomer who in the 9th century calculated the length of the year as being 365 days, 5 hours, 48 minutes and 24 seconds, (in the year 2000 it was calculated to be 365 days, 5 hours, 48 minutes and 45 seconds), and produced work in that field of such import that he was later quoted by Copernicus, Kepler and Galileo, he is included here for his pioneering work in trigonometry.

By the 10th century, Islamic mathematicians were using all six trigonometric functions, had created tables of their values, and were applying them to problems in spherical geometry. Al-Battani was the first person to use in his works the expression "sine" and "cosine" (*watar ma yabqa li-taman*). He discovered trigono-metrical ratios, and improved Ptolemy's astronomical calculations by replacing geometrical methods with trigonometry. He used ingenuous solutions for some problems of spherical trigonometry using methods of orthographic projection. He used trigonometric ratios as we use them today and was the first scientist who replaced the use of Greek chords by sines, as well as developing the concept of the cotangent.

The problem of the classification of Muslim scientists is perhaps particularly striking when we move to the 11th century and look at **Omar Khayyam** (1044–1123 CE). In the West he is best remembered as the author of the *Rubaiyat*, a collection of poems, or quatrains, by the Persian poet, which were famously translated into English by Edward Fitzgerald. His other achievements, however, can be gauged by the fact that it was as a mathematician, in 1079, he calculated the length of the solar year to be 365.24219858156 days, inaccurate by fractions of a second as compared to the 365.242190 calculated in the 21st century with the aid of the Hubble space telescope. In fact, his "year" was more accurate than that of the Gregorian calendar which followed 500 years later and which we still use today. Khayyam was a mathematician, astronomer and physicist who, among his works authored the Treatise on the Demonstration of Problems of Algebra in which we find the first complete treatment of the solution of cubic equations. Yet despite his undoubted mathematical talents he also wrote the *Shark –i Mushkil min Kitab al-Musiqi* in which he found time to deal with the mathematical structures of music.

It can be seen how so often the greatest mathematicians of the Muslim world were also its greatest astronomers. Even this, however, is an unduly restrictive description bearing in mind that it was extremely rare, in fact, that such scholars would restrict themselves to just one or two subjects. Astronomy was a regular specialism of these scholars, perhaps in no small part due to the Quran, which exhorted them to observe the stars in the sky. And observe they did. One of the greatest Muslim astronomers was the polymath Abu Rayhan **al-Biruni** (973–1048 CE) and although almost half of his 146 works were about mathematics and astronomy, his other works highlighted his expert contributions as an anthropologist, geographer, ethnographer, physicist and pharmacologist. As a geographer, for example, he detailed the processes of determining longitude and latitude in his *Taḥdidnihāyāt al-amākin li-taṣḥiḥmasāfātal al-masākin (Determination of the Coordinates of Places for the Correction of Distances Between Cities)*, as well as discussing the formation of mountains and fossils.

As an astronomer, one of al-Biruni's greatest contributions was in drawing the distinction between astronomy and astrology. The latter was immensely popular at the time but al-Biruni, in his *Al-Tafhīm li-awā'ilṣinā'at al-tanjīm (Elements of Astrology)*, showed his very real reservations about the subject, preferring instead the more rational arguments found in astronomy. He devoted most of his work to mathematics, astronomy and geography as well as the manufacture of the astrolabe. As long ago as the 11th century he was arguing that it might be possible for the Earth to rotate on its own axis. In 1000 CE he wrote on calendars and in 1030 he wrote his masterpiece on astronomy, *Qanun al Masudi Fil Haiwal-Najum*, a truly encyclopaedic work of science, which contains collections of 23 observations of equinoxes beginning with observations made by Ptolemy and ending with original observations of his own. In this book he also discussed several theorems of astronomy, trigonometry, solar, lunar and planetary motions.

Another important astronomer and all round scholar in the Islamic world was Muhammad ibn Nasir al-Din **al-Tusi** (1201–1274). By now, perhaps somewhat predictably in our journey through these scholars, we find that al-Tusi numbered among his areas of expertise, philosophy, mathematics, medicine and biology but he is best remembered for his contributions in astronomy. He was born in Persia when it was about to fall victim to the invading Mongols. Al-Tusi, however, subsequently accepted a position to be the Mongol Hulagu Khan's scientific advisor and it was from this influential role that he was able to successfully lobby for the funding for an observatory to be built at Maragheh, the Ilkhanate capital, in modern day Azerbaijan. This was not only an observatory but also one of the foremost libraries in the thirteenth century and became a crucial centre from which knowledge was traded with the Chinese. (It was from this observatory that al-Shirazi later gave an accurate explanation for the phenomenon of the rainbow, an explanation that was further expanded upon by his student al-Farisi.)

From Maragheh, al-Tusi was able to produce the zij Ilkhani (Ilkhan astronomical tables), which were relied upon for centuries thereafter due to their accuracy. Al-Tusi was a prolific writer and it was his *Al –Tadhkira fi 'ilm al Hayah (Treatise on Astronomy)* which contained an astronomical-mathematical breakthrough which came to be known as the Tusi Couple. This re-evaluated and improved upon the ancient planetary models of Ptolemy by creating a system in which all planetary orbits were described by uniform circular motion. Its significance can be seen in the fact that it paved the way for the later work of Copernicus and references to it can be found in his writings. Also in al-Tusi's treatise we find a description of the Milky Way as containing a "very large number of small, tightly-clustered stars, which, on account of their concentration and smallness, seem to be cloudy patches, because of this, it was likened to milk in colour". This composition of the Milky Way was later proved by Galileo.

Al-Tusi derived his appellation from the fact that he was born in Tus in Persia but he was not the only notable Muslim scholar from that ancient city. Some five hundred years earlier **Jabir ibn Hayyan** (721–815), whose name was later Latinized to Geber, was born there and achieved such renown that many regard him as the father of modern chemistry. Although there appears to be considerable dispute as to the exact authorship of many of the works attributed to him, (the later appearance of "pseudo-Geber" does not help in this regard), there seems little doubt that he made significant contributions to the development of chemistry in the western world. He placed great emphasis on the empirical method stating that, "the first essential in chemistry is that you should perform practical work and conduct experiments", and it was this approach that paved the way for the eventual departure of chemistry from the less scientific and more esoteric alchemy. This theme was picked up by his successor and renowned philosopher Yaqub ibn Ishaq **al-Kindi** (800–873) who opposed the views, prevailing in alchemy, that believed in the transformation of base metals into precious ones. Various distillation processes are attributed to Jabir ibn Hayyan as well as the discovery of nitric acid and hydrochloric acid, and also a substantial furthering of the knowledge and use of the alkali (al-Qaly) and alembic (al-inbiq). But as with many Muslim scientists his works were not just theoretical discussions but, in fact, had very practical applications. He was an expert in applied science and was an innovator in areas as diverse as hair dyeing and the rust proofing of metals.

Perhaps, however, the greatest legacy of Muslim scientists was left in the field of medicine. It is no exaggeration to say that for centuries it was the work of Muslim physicians that was regarded as the supreme authority when it came to the treatment of physical ailments. The few such physicians we shall consider span the ninth to the 13th centuries although this by no means marked the parameters of their influence. The first of our examples, and the greatest according to some critics, was the Persian Muhammad ibn Zakaria **al-Razi** (864–930 CE). He is reputed to have authored some 200 works on all aspects of medicine and his fame includes being responsible for a number of significant "firsts" in his chosen field. For example, he is regarded as the first to scientifically describe, and distinguish between, smallpox and measles in his *Kitab al-Judari w'al Hasabah* (The Book of Smallpox and Measles). He was the first to write about allergies and immunology, discovering as he did allergic asthma. He provided the first medical manual for the general public and was the first to use opium for anaesthetic purposes. These were all incredible achievements for his time but, just as importantly, if not more so, he ought to be remembered for his actual approach to his profession. He was unrelenting in his attacks on those he regarded as medical charlatans (which, to be fair, was probably most of those professing to know about medicine in the ninth century), and was insistent that there be a scientific basis for any proposed cures. This emphasis of his went hand in hand with his enthusiasm for continuing professional development and insistence on medical ethics.

There developed various centres of scientific excellence in the Muslim world. Major cities such as Damascus, Cairo and Baghdad became established as places of great learning as well as practical application of their findings. Further west in Spain, Cordoba in the 10th century was described as the "ornament of the world", and not surprisingly it was the birthplace of many a scholar, not just the Muslims we are presently concerned with, but also such luminaries as the Jewish scholar Moses Maimonides. It could also boast as one of its sons, Abu al Qasim **al Zahrawi** (936–1013 CE), known as Albucasis in the West, and regarded by many as the "father of modern surgery". He was an expert in dentistry, pharmacy, and general surgery, but some of his most famous achievements were in the area of obstetrics. He was the first physician to describe an ectopic pregnancy. He also invented a pair of obstetric forceps used to remove a foetus which had perished in the womb, a device which is still in use today, as reported by surgeons at the present day Cordoba Hospital.

Al-Zahrawi was also the author of the leading textbook on surgery in Europe for some five centuries, the Method of Medicine, or the *Kitab al-Tasrif*, which was translated by Gerard of Cremona in the 12th century. This work was made up of thirty-volumes, which included the first accurate description of haemophilia. He was also responsible for the first documentation of the pathology of hydrocephalus. It was Al-Zahrawi who deserved the credit for procedures that took on the names of those who came many centuries after him. For example, he was the first to describe an obstetric delivery position, which later came to be known as the "Walcher position", named after the nineteenth century German obstetrician. Similarly, the 19th-century Swiss physician Emil Kocher, lends his name to a procedure to reduce the anterior dislocation of the shoulder when, in actual fact, the "Kocher manoeuvre" was described in al-Zahrawi's al-Tasrif over a thousand years earlier. Among his other pioneering work we find that he was the first to use catgut sutures, the first to undertake exploratory surgery, as well as being an early proponent of mastectomies.

One, perhaps slightly unconventional, method of recording the fame of medieval scholars is to name a crater on the Moon after them. Abu Ali al-Hasan Ibn **al-Haytham** (965–1040 CE), known as Alhazen in the West, was one such contributor to the naming of lunar craters. Although he is generally described as a polymath responsible for major achievements in several scientific fields, for present purposes, it is his contribution in the field of optics that commands our attention. He authored over 200 works but his seven volumes on optics laid the foundations for the mathematical and optical theories later used by Galileo and Copernicus. (Interestingly he too, was aware of, and applied theories, which subsequently gained appellations derived from the names of others. In his case it was Wilson's theorem, named after the eighteenth century English mathematician.)

Ibn al-Haytham was the first scientist to argue that vision is a phenomenon taking place in the brain rather than in the eyes. Contrary to the thinking prevailing at the time, he proved that light rays do not emanate from the eyeball of the viewer and, indeed, went on to provide one of the earliest accurate descriptions of how the eyeball in fact works. He also proved that light travels in straight lines and such was his understanding of this field that he began to build a camera obscura some five centuries before Leonardo da Vinci. (Incidentally, the law of refraction, also known as Snell's Law or Descartes' Law, after the Dutch astronomer Willebrord Snellius, and the French scientist Descartes, both of whom lived in the seventeenth century, was in fact first accurately described by Ibn Sahl in tenth-century Baghdad.)

A few years after the birth of al-Haytham in what is now Iraq, another child was born not too far away in Iran. He was to go on to be described as "the most famous scientist of Islam" and his full name was Abu 'Ali al-Ḥusayn ibn ʿAbd Allah **ibn Sina** (980–1037 CE), known as Avicenna in the West. He was another polymath who subsequently had the, by now almost mandatory, lunar crater named after him, and having memorized the Quran by the age of 10, he went on to distinguish himself primarily in the fields of medicine, mathematics and philosophy. In medicine his major works included the Book of Healing (*Kitab al-Shifa*) and the Canon of Medicine (*Al Qanoon fi-al Tibb* or the Laws of Medicine). The latter was a fourteen-volume work, which became the standard medical textbook in Europe for some five centuries and was being used in French universities as late as the 17th century. It contained scientific explanations and classifications of diseases at a time when Europe insisted that they were due to Divine punishment. It was translated into Latin by Gerard of Cremona in the 12th century and was published in Venice in 1493 and Rome in 1593 and was being used at the famous medical school of Salerno.

Ibn Sina was another Muslim scientist who insisted on clinical trials and experimentation, and provided the study and practice of medicine with a formal scientific structure. He too refuted alchemy and astrology, preferring instead the more logical and empirical approaches of chemistry and astronomy. He established scientific rules for the testing of drugs, and, so thorough were they, that they still form the basis of clinical pharmacology a thousand years later. He is regarded by many as being the first to formally explain the spread of contagious diseases and the use of quarantine. He emphasized clinical trials and at a time when most of Europe rejected the view, he was insistent that tuberculosis was infectious. He also began the first documented explorations of what later became known as psychotherapy in his discussions of the mind-body connection and the role of mental issues in physical ailments. He gave descriptions of meningitis, discussed anaesthetics and elaborated upon bone fractures and how best to heal them. Once again we find that his work was not purely theoretical but extended to the invention of medical instruments such as the one he used to probe the tear duct.

Ibn Sina undoubtedly left behind an enduring legacy but one scholar who had the stature to criticise his more speculative assertions was Abu Marwan Abd –al-Malik **Ibn Zuhr**(1091–1161 CE), known as Avenzoar in the West. He was born in Seville and graduated from the medical university at Cordoba. Unlike most of the Muslim scholars whom we have considered, Ibn Zuhr confined himself to just one discipline, medicine, but this enabled him to excel as a clinician, physician and parasitologist. He was the first to comprehensively describe parasites and the diseases they caused such as scabies. He knew the human anatomy in detail, having become an expert at the dissection of cadavers. He was also the first to test different medicines on animals before administering them to humans. His experimentation on animals, in particular goats, also led to his formalizing and perfecting the practice of tracheotomies and direct feeding through the gullet where normal feeding was not possible. Although he was the author of many works, only three of his major books remain, the *Book of Simplification Concerning Therapeutics and Diet*, the catchily-titled *Book of the Middle Course Concerning the Reformation of Souls and Bodies*, and the more manageable *Book of Foodstuffs*. Aside from his medical achievements he should also be remembered for persuading his daughter and grand-daughter to go into medicine, perhaps a surprising initiative, given that he lived in the 12th century, which some Muslims would do well to now adopt in the 21st.

Ibn Zuhr was also notable for being a teacher of the great Averroes, or Abu'l Walid **Ibn Rushd** (1128–1198 CE). His is a name, which is certainly known in the West and along with Ibn Sina he even "merited" a place in Limbo in Dante's *Divine Comedy*. He is mainly remembered for his philosophical work, and, in particular, his rationalist approach, which dramatically altered the landscape of Western thought five centuries before the thinking of Rene Descartes. He did, however, originally study medicine and law and his major work on medicine was *Al-Kulliyyat* or *Generalities,* which was translated into Latin as the *Colliget*. This was done in Padua in 1255 CE and the first edition was printed in Venice in 1492 CE. It is subdivided into seven further books, the *Anatomy of Organs, Health, Sickness, Symptoms, Drugs and Foods, Hygiene and Therapy*, and together with Ibn Zuhr's work on Therapeutics and Diet, it was intended to form a comprehensive alternative medical text to Ibn Sina's Canon. Despite having authored a commentary on the Canon, Ibn Rushd will always be remembered first and foremost as a philosopher rather than a physician but this should in no way detract from his contribution to medicine, particularly in Muslim Spain.

The final character we shall mention when perusing Islamic scientific achievements is Ala al-Din **Ibn Nafis** (1213–1288 CE) who was born in Damascus and went on to become the head of Cairo hospital. He, too, wrote commentaries on the work of the great scholars of medicine such Ibn Sina and Hunan Ibn Ishaq, as well as producing his own treatises on ophthalmology, eye diseases and diet. It was in his commentary on Ibn Sina's Canon that we find the first description of pulmonary circulation, i.e. the movement of blood from the heart to the lungs and back to the heart again, with Ibn Nafis correcting the hitherto accepted view, originating from the Greek physician Galen, that blood passed directly from the right side of the heart to the left. Ibn Nafis stated that the wall between the right and left ventricles of the heart was non-porous and that the blood must, therefore, pass between the right and left ventricle by way of the lungs.

It has been widely held this view was first promulgated in Europe by Michael Servetus in 1553, Andreas Vesalius in 1555 and Realdus Columbo in 1559, who were all precursors to William Harvey, whose publication in 1628 is regarded as the definitive discovery of blood circulation. At its most charitable, this version of history holds that the European "discovery" was independent of Ibn Nafis' earlier work, of which it was completely in the dark.

This view may be accurate but it bears a little more scrutiny as it also has a bearing on our wider discussion of the significance of Muslim scientific achievements. The relevant text by Ibn Nafis was found in the Prussian State Library in 1924 and the assertion has always been that it could not have been known by the European scholars. History does record, however, that there was an Italian physician from Belluno near Padua by the name of Andrea Alpago, who lived in Syria for some time where he encountered the work of Ibn Nafis, who we recall was born in Damascus. He translated this into Latin and it was published in Venice in 1547, some 25 years after he had died. Michael Servetus had spent time in Italy and in 1553 published *Christianismi Restitutio*, the *Restoration of Christianity*, in which he put forward the theory of pulmonary circulation. As its name suggests, however, this work was a theological work and a highly controversial one at that, in as much as it was regarded as anti-Trinitarian and heretical, and was, therefore, destroyed. Few copies remained, so unsurprisingly, the pulmonary circulation part did not gain too much publicity.

In 1555 Andreas Vesalius, a Flemish anatomist, published a revised edition of his work *De Humani Corporis Fabrica (On the Fabric of the Human Body)*, in which he disputed Galen's view that the wall between the ventricles of the heart was porous. Vesalius had also lived briefly in Venice before moving to Padua to study for his doctorate, which he received in 1537, and, after which, he became the Chair of Surgery and Anatomy at the University. A colleague, or perhaps more likely, a rival, of Vesalius at Padua was Realdo Colombo who was a surgeon and professor of anatomy at Padua from 1544 to 1559. He also shares the title of the "discoverer" of pulmonary circulation, as does a student of his called Juan Valverde de Amusco. One of the interesting facts relating to these three scholars of Padua is the mutual accusations of plagiarism, which were exchanged between them. Now it may seem at first blush that the work of the Englishman William Harvey, published in 1628, was entirely unconnected to, and independent of, these Italian shenanigans, until, that is, we discover that

Harvey himself studied at the University of Padua between 1599 and 1602. It may well be the case that the work of Ibn Nafis did, in fact, remain unknown to Europe until 1924 and the fortuitous find in the Prussian Library. It is also at least possible, however, that his work had filtered through to the universities of Italy and from there been disseminated elsewhere.

Perhaps this brings us neatly to the point about the significance of the above-mentioned Muslim scientific achievements. The purpose of this chapter was never to bask in the shade of past glories, but, first and foremost, to educate and inform. This, itself, is not a task which is directed just at non-Muslims but also to Muslims themselves who are, all too often, sadly unaware of their own history, and the achievements which can properly be attributed to their ancestors. It is, nevertheless, painful to bring to mind just how little of the above history is taught in western schools and it requires no great intellectual leap to anticipate what the results of this lack of information are likely to be. Science is portrayed as the preserve of the civilized West, with the rest of the world, particularly the Muslim world, lagging behind. And, of course, implicit in this notion is the belief that it was always thus. Muslim children grow up not realising that their ancestors made huge contributions to the cause of science, and non-Muslim children see no alternative to the negative stereotypes regularly depicted by the media. For this reason alone it is vital that Islamic scientific achievements are recalled and highlighted.

When undertaking this task it soon becomes apparent that there are some underlying themes that are worth noting. Perhaps the most important is the fact that it is not merely coincidental that Muslim scientific success often occurred in places where there was political stability and material wealth. There was an undoubted thirst for knowledge but quenching it was made all the easier by the fact that there were wealthy and powerful rulers who were willing to sponsor those engaged in academic endeavour. Perhaps inevitably, once centres of learning were established in cities from Cordoba in the West, to Samarkand in the East, taking in Cairo, Damascus and Baghdad along the way, they were bound to attract the greatest minds, secure in the belief that their efforts would be fully supported. Similarly, today, we note how the cause of scientific progress is furthered most in those countries that, not only have the means to fund it, but are also able to provide the physical security and political stability for those intent on pursuing it. It is no accident that in contemporary Muslim societies, most scientific progress takes place in countries such as Turkey and Malaysia, where there is relative prosperity and political stability.

Another theme that we can see when we peruse the history of Islamic scientific success is the extent to which there was cross-pollination of ideas. In the days before copyright and patent issues became so prominent, it was the accepted belief, certainly among Muslims, that there should be no monopoly over knowledge, the Creator having made it freely available to all who sought it. Muslim scholars readily absorbed the works of the Greeks and Indians, and the technology of the Persians and Chinese, and regarded it as their duty to develop this knowledge and pass it on to others. Although the description "Arabic" numerals, for example, has come to be accepted now, a thousand years ago the Arabs themselves, referred to the numbers as Indian or Hindi, thereby acknowledging where they had inherited this knowledge from.

Yet the notion of sharing knowledge was not just apparent when it came to accepting received wisdom. Perhaps the best example of this is the success story of Al-Andalus, or Muslim Spain, a thousand or so years ago. Cordoba was a city, which at one time, was probably the biggest, cleanest, most learned and technically advanced in the world. A major part of its success, however, was rooted in the fact that it provided an environment where mutual co-operation between Muslims, Christians and Jews was valued and encouraged. Thus it is that it becomes the city that produced no less a Jewish scholar than Moses Maimonides, and in Ibn Rushd or Averroes, a Muslim philosopher whose commentaries on Aristotle significantly influenced the thinking of Thomas Aquinas. (Perhaps it is also worth noting, albeit regrettably, that their respective communities criticised each of these scholars for their inclusive outlook.)

The most important, and, at the same time most controversial, idea which we gain from this journey through the scientific successes of medieval Muslims, however, is that relating to the role that such successes played in the creation of the modern West. We are all familiar with the usage of the phrase "Arabic numerals" and know why our numbers are described as Arabic. We are perhaps less aware, however, of the origins of words such as algebra, zero, cipher, almanac, zenith, azimuth, alchemy, alcohol, alkali, elixir, syrup, bazaar, tariff and arsenal. All of these words have their origins in the world of Islam, and it is perhaps important to note here the significance of language in the development of civilisations and cultures. Only a moment's thought about the cultural supremacy which the West holds over the world today, and the role that the English language plays in this, is sufficient to make our point. There is a reason why these Arabic words found their way in to western languages, and it is simply this: they comprised the vocabulary of the academics and experts who were discussing the major ideas of the day.

It was not just words, however, which the Muslims provided for the West. We have already noted how certain ideas that were later adopted by Europeans, did in fact, originate in earlier Islamic thought. The names of William Harvey, Snell, Walcher and Kocher, may be the ones we recall but that should not make us blind to the fact that much original thinking in scientific fields had been going on for centuries before they emerged on the scene. To be fair, often the Western scholars themselves were happy to acknowledge the efforts of their predecessors, but it was their followers who gave the impression that Western achievements were born out of an intellectual vacuum. Our discussions of astronomy may begin and end with Copernicus but the man himself was happy to quote Al-Battani and Ibn al-Haytham.

We may believe that one of the great achievements of western civilization was to rid the scientific world of the irrational religious superstitions, which hampered its progress, but again the reality is somewhat different. Muslim scientist after Muslim scientist emphasized the importance of experimentation and the empirical method. Similarly, the backlash of the Church against science was not a phenomenon familiar to the Muslim scholars who, on the contrary, were actively encouraged by their faith in their scientific pursuits.

CHAPTER 5

Or in Need of Anger Management?

Muslims seem to be an angry bunch don't they? There is a perception, perhaps understandable to some extent, that all Muslims ever do is gripe, moan, demonstrate, protest and ultimately lash out violently. Unreasonable and uncivilised, they contrive to cover up their own shortcomings by constantly blaming others. This applies collectively as well as individually. Muslim countries always blame "the West" for their problems without ever mentioning the corruption, lack of political freedoms and wanton violence, amongst other flaws, which characterise their own societies. Muslims, as individuals, adopt a persecution complex where they are always the victims of discrimination because of their religion. Wilfully cutting themselves off from the rest of society, they inevitably lose out on opportunities which may otherwise present themselves, and they then resort to attributing the cause of their ills to the actions of others. The undercurrent of such negative perceptions of Muslims is, of course, that it is the actions of Muslims themselves that are the problem, as they have no legitimate basis whatsoever. Is this, however, entirely true? Are Muslims completely unreasonable or are some of their grievances real, and their complaints justified? These are some of the questions which merit further consideration to ascertain whether or not Muslims need to be collectively booked on to some anger-management courses.

It is very rare that I bemoan the state of the Islamic world in the 21st century and blame it on the Crusades, but there is a feeling, expressed by some, that Muslims have very long memories and have neither forgotten, nor forgiven, the Christian Crusaders who invaded the Middle East. The events may well have taken place almost a thousand years ago but they are supposedly etched very clearly in the minds of all Muslims, and explain the resentment of the West in the Muslim world. Well, in case anybody is wondering, I am not holding the Crusades against my Christian friends, nor am I waiting for any form of redress. The Crusades were undoubtedly a tragic chapter in the history of Christian-Muslim relations but they are not a regular topic of conversation in Muslim households. At least they were not until George W. Bush famously used the word prior to invading Iraq, thereby reminding Muslims that even if they had forgotten the Crusades, the descendants of those who were responsible for them certainly had not.

When Pope Urban II called for the Crusades in 1095 he set off a train of events that was to leave an indelible mark on the Middle East. At the time, Christianity was split between the eastern Byzantine Church and the western Latin Church, and, it is fair to say that there was not necessarily a great deal of trust between the two. The Crusades were one way for the Pope to gain supremacy over the whole of the Church by ending the savage persecution of Christians by the infidel Muslims, and regaining Jerusalem in the process. The problem with this, however, was that there was no savage persecution of Christians by Muslims. Jerusalem had been in Muslim hands for almost 500 years and in that time the majority of the population had remained Christian. At a stage in history when general slaughter was not uncommon, it may be regarded as somewhat surprising that Muslims did not compel the Christians of Jerusalem to convert to Islam or face the sword, but this fact only reflects the religious tolerance enjoined upon them in the Quran where they are reminded that there is "no compulsion in faith". The ruling Muslims, the Fatimids of Egypt, were fairly tolerant for their time, but this was happily overlooked by the Pope, and those who followed his command were barely concerned with the niceties of religious faith, as was amply manifested in their conduct en route to the Holy Land when they attacked fellow Christians as well as, sadly rather more predictably, any Jewish communities they encountered. Once they eventually arrived in Jerusalem, the manner in which they took the city was so unnecessarily brutal that the accounts of their horses being knee deep in the bodies of "infidel" men, women and children (and animals), bear testimony to this day.

There then followed a Crusader presence in the Holy Land for hundreds of years. In that time, however, there was some regrouping and eventual reconquests by the Muslims, the most famous of which were the efforts of Saladin, and his capture of Jerusalem in 1187. It is also fair to observe that some of these reconquests were not exactly met with displeasure by the local Eastern

Christians. They may well have believed in the same Christ as their Latin brethren, but they looked and behaved similarly to their Muslim counterparts and this was a fact, which had not pleased the newly arrived Crusaders and certainly did not increase the trust between the two branches of the faith. (Even today the Coptic Christians of Egypt refer to God as Allah, and one wonders how they would be received by the evangelical right wing of Christianity in the West.)

Saladin is, of course, a hero to Muslims for his recapture of Jerusalem but he is also legendary in the West as a chivalrous warrior. He was famed for his generosity and humanity, releasing prisoners of war at a time when it was customary to execute them. Richard the Lionheart himself, for example, ordered the massacre of 2,700 survivors of the Muslim garrison of Acre. This perceived distinction between the conduct of Muslims and Christians during the period of the Crusades is one of the legacies of this chapter of history, certainly as far as Muslims are concerned. They contrast the way in which Saladin captured Jerusalem, leaving unharmed all women and children, with the manner in which it fell in 1099 and the wanton bloodshed that followed at the hands of the invading Crusaders.

It serves the purposes of some, however, in both the Muslim and Christian camp, to depict the Crusades as a war between Islam and Christianity itself. They insist that the two faiths could not happily co-exist and that violence was the only solution in order to find out which one should dominate. This type of view has always been resisted by others who happen to share the faith, who regard God as the ultimate arbiter of religious disputes, rather than those who carry the bigger sticks. Invariably, what such people also recognised was the fact that, more often than not, so-called "religious" disputes were a convenient way of disguising wars, which had other motives. Pope Urban II's motives were not as simple as protecting the faith, any more than the motives of the Crusaders themselves. We find these themes recurring constantly in history, where some sort of pretext (often downright lies and distortions), is used as a cover for wars that are essentially motivated by considerations of political power and greed. Similarly, the Crusades themselves were, in fact, motivated by political and financial considerations, as well as being wars of colonisation where the colonisers were seeking to impose their civilisation on the subjected populations. They were not the first such wars, nor would they be the last, especially as far as Muslims were concerned, who in due course would become all too familiar with subjugation by European Christians.

Almost every Muslim country was colonised by the Western powers at some stage and this was a situation, which for many such countries did not change until the last fifty years or so. What this has meant is that for many Muslims, obviously the experiences of colonisation are much more relevant than those of the Crusades. They were experiences that not only left a legacy in those countries, but also continue to influence the relationship between Muslims and the West today. For example, the centuries-long involvement of the British in India ultimately led to the immigration to the United Kingdom of Pakistani workers, amongst others, in the post war years. (And without that immigration, this book would not have been written.) Similar patterns can be witnessed in other European countries. France had a colonial presence in Algeria from 1830 to 1962, as well as in Tunisia and Morocco, leading to its large North African immigrant population today. It subsequently colluded with the British in the partitioning of the Ottoman Empire and French influence is still visible today in Lebanon where it carried out its "divide and rule" policy with some success. Britain's history of involvement in the region includes a period of direct military control of Iraq as well as the later installation of kings it regarded as suitable for its purposes, which, of course, were not necessarily the purposes of the host nation. The British also had significant control of Egypt, including periods of indirect rule when the apparent leader may have been the emir, sheikh or khedive, but the true power lay elsewhere.

Contemporary global events highlight some interesting parallels with the colonial period of history, as well as numerous lessons that perhaps ought to have been learned. Iraq is the obvious example where we continue to intervene with scant regard for the wishes, or indeed the lives, of the indigenous population. The first Iraq war in 1991 is now regarded as legally and morally justified, (in part because the later one was so obviously not), yet few people remember the role that April Glaspie played prior to the Iraqi invasion of Kuwait, which led to Western intervention. She was the American ambassador to Iraq and prior to invading Kuwait, Saddam Hussein held a meeting with her. During the course of that meeting he mentioned to her the "difficulty" he was having with Kuwait, there being allegations by the Iraqis that the Kuwaitis were illegally drilling for oil in Iraqi fields. The response from her was that as far as the United States was concerned it was an internal matter for the Iraqis, one upon which the USA had "no opinion".

One could well understand that Saddam Hussein being an ally of the United States, having attacked Iran at the instigation of the United States, having been armed by the United States, interpreted this response as a green light from his ally. Yet what followed thereafter was unprecedented in the speed and scale of the military action against him. Numerous opportunities to forestall war were spurned by America who seemed intent on taking this opportunity to destroy Iraq's military capability whilst testing out its own. Perhaps the most sickening episode of this war was the "turkey shoot" towards the end of the conflict, when American soldiers happily gloated about wiping out thousands of *fleeing* Iraqi soldiers. One wonders how such events would have been reported had matters been the other way round.

The approach to the invasion of 2003 clearly involved many more economies of truth than were required in 1991, but certain features remained the same. Naomi Klein in *The Shock Doctrine* highlights how profits accrued to the same western corporations, $20 billion worth of contracts to Halliburton alone. (Setting aside moral considerations for a moment, one can marvel at the genius of a system which generates huge profits by selling arms to make nations powerful, generates huge profits by using arms to destroy the nations made so powerful, and then generates huge profits from the contracts to rebuild the same nations after such destruction. "Win-win" does not even begin to describe this state of affairs.)

Another feature that remained the same in 2003 as in 1991 was the callous indifference for those whom we claimed to be seeking to save. Western championing of the Kurds was part of the build-up to the invasion of Iraq in 2003, yet, just as before, once our immediate objective was achieved, that Kurdish homeland remained as elusive for the Kurds as it always had been. At this point it is perhaps worth remembering the words of General F.S. Maude, Commander of British Forces, Baghdad, March 19th 1917. *"Our armies do not come into your cities and lands as conquerors or enemies, but as liberators...it is the hope and desire of the British people and the nations in alliance with them that the Arab race may rise once more to greatness and renown among the peoples of the earth."* The professed enthusiasm for "liberating" was presumably not intended to mean liberating their resources. That was just a happy coincidence.

Events in Iraq showed how, so often, rulers in the Middle East are installed and removed at our behest, no matter what kind of democratic veneer is applied by our politicians in order to stave off domestic criticism. In the past some of these Muslim countries looked to the West for support in achieving their own reforms and independence, for example from the Ottomans, but then, as now, our support for democratic reforms did not take precedence over our colonial/national interests. From early 2011 a wave of pro-democracy demonstrations took place in Muslim countries from Tunisia to Syria, yet Western support was tempered to say the least, dependent on our interests, rather than those of the demonstrators. NATO intervention in Libya, for example, was viewed with suspicion as being based on our hatred of Gaddafi and/or love of his oil, rather than any democratic principle, and was always going to be contrasted with the policy of encouraging "stability" when similar anti-government demonstrations had taken place earlier in Egypt.

The number of civilian deaths that have occurred in Iraq from the time of the invasion in 2003 is estimated to be in the region of one million. The fact we do not know the exact figure is because no such record has ever been maintained (contrary to the norms of conduct in war), and this sorry fact is seen to reflect the general lack of interest that the West has always shown towards the populations of such countries. It was Winston Churchill who once made the infamous remark about not getting unduly squeamish about the use of chemical weapons on "savage tribes". He was a true British hero but, given that remark, it may come as no surprise that others around the world regard him with some antipathy. Churchill was referring to the use of such weapons on the people of Iraq, yet no irony was noted when the very same chemical weapons were used as part of the pretext to justify the Iraq invasion. It is, of course, now old news that such weapons of mass destruction did not, in fact, exist in Iraq immediately prior to the invasion. They certainly found their way to Iraq once the Western war effort was in full swing, however, as evidenced by their use by the "coalition" in Fallujah. This appalling episode received little attention in the West and again begged the question by many Muslims of how it would have been treated by the media if the victims had been non-Muslims in Europe or America. The suspicion in many quarters was that it would have received saturation coverage (although when Saddam Hussein himself used chemical weapons on the people of Halabja during the Iran-Iraq war, our condemnation was somewhat muted, perhaps understandably, given the fact that he was then our ally and it was we who had armed him).

One would expect Muslims to feel aggrieved at being colonised or subjected to unwarranted military occupation or action. These were visible interventions, which were more acceptable in an age when many Western powers were behaving similarly. Times change however, and in the post-war years imperialist ventures and colonialism came to be depicted as a thing of the past. Many countries of the developing world began to gain independence and on the face of it this was ushering in an era of autonomy and self-determination. Some would argue however, that all that changed was that direct intervention became indirect, and physical colonisation was replaced by cultural and economic colonisation. After all, why go to the expense and inconvenience of physically occupying and ruling a country if there were other ways of relieving it of its resources?

Resources, or in other words wealth, was ultimately what the Western powers were after, and they competed with each other to gain mastery over the wealth of the world, whether in Africa and India in the past, or the Middle East and its oil resources in the present. Intervention, or in the eyes of some, interference, which fell short of direct military occupation, increasingly became the preferred tactic. Tragically, and with a staggering degree of short-sightedness, little attention was paid to the potential consequences of such interventions. So, although the age of colonialism was ending, that did not mean for a moment that foreign lands would be left in control of their own affairs.

Many Muslim countries, particularly in the Middle East, had experienced Western intervention in the form of European colonialism. Britain, France, Germany, Italy and others had a physical presence in such countries, which many Muslims were now glad to see the back of.

They looked forward to independence and took heart from the power visible across the Atlantic Ocean in the form of America. That nation had fought for its own independence from the very same colonialism. It had not itself developed colonies around the world. And, as seen in the 20th century it had on occasion used its military might to safeguard the security of other nations under threat. All this explains how up until the middle of that century, the Muslim world had high regard for the United States, certainly as compared to the other powers which they had encountered in the past. Things were to change drastically for a variety of reasons. We shall look at Israel shortly, as it represents perhaps the greatest grievance that Muslims hold against America, but its case is far from an isolated example of the US getting itself involved in the affairs of Muslims, and indeed, their neighbours. The United States of America may insist it has no imperialist ambitions and may utter all the right words about democracy and freedom, but even a cursory look at its track record suggests that this picture is not entirely accurate.

One of the disadvantages of being part of a western democracy is that our attention is diverted from any conflict between suited politicians saying all the right things, whilst insidious secret services do all the wrong things. In fact, much of the time we, the populace, are totally oblivious to the fact that such secret services play a significant role at all, and are content to accept the headlines at face value. "National security" require-ments mean that documents are classified for decades so it is only much later that a clearer picture finally emerges. This, of course, assumes that those who are still around still have sufficient interest in the topic. The United

States (and other so-called liberal democracies) are then revealed to have often suppressed and opposed many a progressive movement around the globe.

Volumes have been written about the devastation wrought in Latin America with the encouragement and connivance of the US, but for now, it is the Muslim world which is the focus of our attention, and, it is an area which is replete with examples of the Land of the Free subverting democracy and overthrowing regimes. In 1953 for example, democratically elected Iranian prime minister Mossadeq, declared that the oil under Iranian soil belonged to Iran, but failed to realise that such talk was never going to endear him to Uncle Sam who, inevitably, decided it was best to get rid of him. Lest it be thought this was an isolated example, the USA did its best thereafter to ensure that no corner of the Muslim world (or indeed anywhere else) escaped the reach of its tentacles.

The same decade saw attempts to overthrow the Syrian government as well as concerted efforts to overthrow or even assassinate Nasser of Egypt. (The British and French, in collusion with Israel, also thought that the latter was a legitimate target and I still remember my shock at reading the *Observer's* report in 1986 of Anthony Eden's role in the attempt against Nasser's life. Evidently the 30-year-rule could hide some pretty dastardly deeds). There were Arab nationalist leaders at the time who attempted to remain neutral in the Cold War but as far as the United States was concerned there was no such thing as remaining neutral; you were either pro-American or you were communist. Any nationalist sentiments were, by definition, not pro-American and, according to American logic, therefore, must have been communist. This anti-communist paranoia created much death and destruction around the world and Muslim countries were not exempt. General Kassem in Iraq had overthrown the monarchy and established a republic. He desired to remain neutral in the Cold War but in helping to create OPEC (the Organisation of Petroleum Exporting Countries which undermined Western control over the marketing of the Middle East's oil) he had clearly indicated that he was serving the wrong national interest. This was sufficient for the British and Americans to back a coup against him.

It was anti-communist feeling that motivated American policy in Indonesia too, home to the world's largest population of Muslims. Sukarno became the first Indonesian president in 1949 having previously been the leader of the movement to gain independence from the Netherlands. He nationalized many private holdings of the Dutch and in his efforts illustrated that he put the interests of his own countrymen first. Despite their expressed intentions to counter communism, it is evident from their actions that the Americans primary goal was as ever, to disrupt any socially progressive movement, which may send out the wrong signals to others. All around the world the USA was seen to intervene wherever it felt that its business interests would suffer if the locals insisted on working to further their own interests, namely improving their quality of life, usually at the expense of western corporations. Despite Sukarno jointly founding the Non-Aligned Movement, (the clue is in the name) which attempted to remain neutral in the American-Soviet conflict, he was setting an example that the US could not tolerate. In 1966 he was overthrown by General Suharto and the mass killing of "communists" ensued, assisted in part by the US embassy helpfully providing lists of said communists to the army.

In the 1970s the United States participated in its occasional pastime of supporting the Kurds. The Kurdish people are predominantly Sunni Muslims who inhabit the area where Turkey, Syria, Iran and Iraq meet. When the Ottoman Empire was carved up, by the Treaty of Sevres in 1920 the Kurds were promised independence, but when Ataturk came to power he rejected the treaty and agreed with Iraq and Iran not to recognise an independent Kurdish state. There then followed decades of their struggle for independence lying dormant whilst their population suffered at the hands of the governments of the region. They found an unexpected ally in the form of the United States but soon found that this was support based upon political expedience rather than any principled desire to see an independent Kurdistan. It was that highly regarded combination of Richard Nixon and Henry Kissinger (hardly renowned for their ethical foreign policy, or ethical anything for that matter) who began to provide military aid to the Kurds of Iraq. This, however, was in order to drain and distract Iraq and, thereby, serve the interests of their regional ally, the Shah of Iran. Once Iran and Iraq had come to terms in 1975, the Kurds were abandoned to their fate, sadly, not for the last time.

The Shah of Iran was a close friend of the West and the US in particular, and he was also a dramatic illustration of how America conducted itself on the world stage. The US had backed the Shah of Iran, as it had many other Middle Eastern dictators, but was so unconcerned with the rest of the Iranian population that it failed to notice that there was a popular movement gaining strength to the extent that it ultimately overthrew the Shah in 1979, with his backers being left powerless. The exiled Ayatollah Khomeini returned a hero and almost overnight a whole country was turned anti-American with repercussions that still reverberate to this day. Following the Iranian Revolution, a CIA "village" was discovered in Tehran, yet one wonders what kind of "intelligence" they were gathering which caused them to miss an entire country turning against its ruler, and inevitably, his international sponsors.

Rather than learn the lessons of that episode, however, the US has continued to involve itself in the affairs of other countries by supporting dictators, coups, and violence whilst being utterly disinterested in the wishes of the populations of those countries. As late as 2013 it was continuing its policy of supporting tiny corrupt elites at the expense of the rest of the country, as long as those elites served their purpose of advancing American interests whilst controlling their domestic populations. The preaching of freedom and democracy continued to ring out, especially when targeted at rival/enemy countries such as China, but when there seemed to be genuine attempts to gain democratic rights in Egypt, for example, the foot dragging on the part of the US was painful to watch. Rather than rejoice in the spontaneous assertion of the Egyptians desire for political freedoms, something which President Obama had openly called for in his address to the Muslims of the world in June 2009, the Americans called for "stability", for which we can read maintaining the pro-American status quo of the dictator Hosni Mubarak.

Over thirty years after the Islamic Revolution in Iran, the CIA continues to act with impunity in neighbouring

Pakistan, content that those in power in that country are compliant, regardless of what the other 180 million people may think. The arrest of suspected CIA operative Raymond Davis in early 2011 for killing two Pakistanis further agitated a nation already frustrated at its impotence in the face of the American aggression perpetrated on its soil, and highlighted just how much licence to operate had been granted to the CIA by the Pakistani authorities. In fact, the Pakistani foreign minister resigned his position rather than give in to American/Pakistani government pressure to change the visa of Raymond Davis to a diplomatic one after he had been arrested. Here was a country, which was an ally in the War on Terror, and had suffered greatly for being so, with some 35,000 people having been killed as of May 2011 (over ten times the death toll of 9/11). Yet, despite this, it was the subject of constant attacks by unmanned American drone aircraft, and was vilified in the western media, regularly being described as a failed state and terrorist hotbed.

Such allegations resurfaced again in May 2011 when Osama Bin Laden was shot dead in Abbotabad in Pakistan. Initial reports were that he was living in a luxury compound, had been armed, had used his wife as a human shield, was shot whilst resisting "arrest", and the whole episode was viewed by President Obama watching a real time live video feed. Within days this version was amended to the luxury compound being just a dwelling with no air conditioning, Bin Laden not being armed, not using his wife as a human shield and the event not being watched by the US president because the live feed was lost for 25 minutes at the crucial time. Such inconsistencies were lost in the fog of accusations being levelled at Pakistan about what it knew and when it knew it. They also did not serve to placate a sceptical Pakistani population, which again felt angered and humiliated at the flagrant breach of their national sovereignty whilst their own government did nothing. The actions of the Americans also did little to convince other Muslims around the globe, who queried, amongst other things, why the most wanted man in the world was not arrested (especially if he was unarmed), why his wife was not detained by the Americans when surely she would have been able to provide much useful information, and why having dumped his body at sea, the Americans insisted this was to do with their concern for Muslim sensibilities. The latter point confirmed for many Muslims, the contempt with which they were regarded by the US.

The media, which we shall look at later, appeared keen to report matters that reflected badly on Pakistan but never to investigate any suggestions that it was also subjected to deliberate attempts to destabilise it. One such suggestion was that the USA was covertly supporting an independence movement in the province of Balochistan. In that classic imperialist tactic of divide and rule, articles would appear in Western journals discussing such movements, thereby lending credence to them. Then financial and military aid would follow in the full knowledge that this would lead to instability at the very least, and if required, provide a pretext for direct military intervention. Of course, as this never made the western press it was deemed not to have occurred, and anybody bold enough to raise it was given no credence. After all, why on earth would the United States undermine its own allies? Those who posed this question seemed blissfully unaware of the America's track record. Not for nothing has it been said that it is dangerous to be America's enemy, but not as dangerous as it is being its friend. The question also ignored the complex geopolitics of the area.

Balochistan is the largest province in Pakistan. It has vast untapped mineral reserves including copper, gold and platinum. It provides one third of Pakistan's gas. It has borders with Iran and Helmand province in Afghanistan. It also contains the port of Gwadar, a Chinese built facility, which allows China's landlocked western provinces access to the sea and, in particular, the oil shipping lanes of the Straits of Hormuz. China could transport goods by road through Pakistan in a day to Gwadar thereby saving itself the considerable time and expense of accessing the sea through its eastern borders. If ever a province was begging for American interference, it was Balochistan. Pakistani military officials, constantly maligned in the West as being treacherous closet extremists, lament the fact that they help the Americans against the Taliban, at great cost to their own nation, and at the same time have to deal with American and Indian support for a separatist movement in Balochistan.

Destabilizing countries in the Islamic world is seen by Muslims, as a tactic which keeps them from developing and helps further the agenda of the imperialists who can continue to proclaim their superiority due to their democratic credentials. Instability provides a ready-made excuse to intervene militarily, as and when required, and of course, helps keep Defence budgets astronomically high, even after the threat from communist Russia has long since subsided. An army of pro-Israel media "experts", particularly in the United States, then uses such instability to help show Israel in a glowing light, surrounded as it is by undemocratic, violent, Muslim nations hell-bent on its destruction. Israel, which was hardly cheering for the Arab Spring in 2011, in turn never ceases to portray itself as the only democracy in the Middle East, conveniently ignoring how the dictator-ships arose in the first place, as well as countries such as Lebanon, or even Iran. The democratic efforts of those countries perhaps help to explain Israel's willingness to either a) invade them, as in its regular destructive jaunts into Lebanon, or; b) make concerted efforts to ensure that somebody else, particularly the US, invades them on its behalf. For years the Israelis have highlighted the "threat" of Iran, this despite the fact that in the 34 years since the Iranian Revolution, Iran has not invaded a single country. The same, of course, cannot be said for Israel, a fact that the Lebanese know only too well. Disappointingly, for Israel, this has yet to result in an American invasion of Iran but it is certainly not for want of Israeli efforts.

The Israeli author Israel Shahak wrote in February 1993, "*Since the spring of 1992 public opinion in Israel is being prepared for the prospect of a war with Iran, to be fought to bring about Iran's total military and political defeat. In one version, Israel would attack Iran alone; in another it would "persuade" the West to do the job. The indoctrination campaign to this effect is gaining in intensity. It is accompanied by what could be called semi-official horror scenarios purporting to detail what Iran could do to Israel and the West and the entire world when it acquires nuclear weapons as it is expected to a few years hence.*" Two decades have passed since these words were written. Iran has attacked nobody and developed no nuclear weapons. Yet the propaganda juggernaut rumbles on.

Of course all of Israel's actions, which meet with international criticism (and there must be enough of them given the number of United Nations resolutions which it has ignored and/or contravened over the years), are justified by it as being necessary for its security. It has never hesitated to describe the stateless, powerless, impoverished Palestinians as a threat to its very existence, despite itself being a nuclear power which has the unparalleled support of a country which continues to arm it and fund it to the tune of $3 billion per annum. It continues to use the most advanced military hardware against defenceless civilians seemingly oblivious to the fact that, since its very inception, Israel has done most of the killing whilst its Palestinian victims have done most of the dying. It continues to bemoan the absence of worthy leaders of the Palestinian cause whilst doing its best to assassinate them (although "targeted killing" is the preferred Israeli euphemism). It has not hesitated to destroy Palestinian educational establishments and then wonder why the Palestinians cannot boast an educated class like Israel. In short it does everything in its power to depict Palestinians as a non-people, clearly undeserving of the dignity and rights that the rest of the civilized world takes for granted.

In tandem with its military actions its public relations onslaught ensures that criticism is kept to a minimum and/or ruthlessly countered. It is always the Palestinians who are shown as the warmongers and obstructers of peace, despite the fact that even intellectuals from a Jewish background, such as Noam Chomsky, have spent decades detailing Palestinian peace initiatives, which were scuppered by Israel. In an age when it is becoming more and more difficult for Israel to conceal its crimes and thereby maintain its mythical status as the powerless lamb about to be devoured by Arab wolves, Israel is becoming increasingly desperate in its actions. The 2006 invasion of Lebanon drew widespread international condemnation, which had absolutely no effect on the Israeli government whatsoever. Only two countries steadfastly refused to call for an immediate ceasefire, the United States and the United Kingdom, thereby reinforcing the belief of many Muslims that Israel was nothing more than the imperialist colonizing venture, which they had suspected all along.

Further Israeli desperation could be seen in the fact that successive governments attempted to outdo each other with their "security", i.e. anti-Palestinian measures and ended up having extremist caricatures leading their nation. One such character is Avigdor Lieberman who continues the long line of fanatically paranoid Israeli politicians who barely regards the Palestinians as human. Benyamin Netanyahu has attempted over the years to temper his extremist urges but still occasionally lets slip what he really thinks of the Palestinians. (It would appear that his contempt for President Obama is only marginally more concealed, although not particularly well when it came to the 2012 Presidential election.) The religious extremists who one would be forgiven for thinking exist only in the Muslim world get barely a mention if they are Israeli. Rabbi Ovadia Yosef can openly say that Hurricane Katrina was due to the godlessness of New Orleans and due to American pressure on Israel to withdraw from Gaza. He can declare that gentiles only exist to serve Jews yet how many of us have ever heard of him?

The impression that emerges, for many Muslims at least, after a cursory glance at the history of Western involvement in Muslim countries is the prevalence of double standards. Democracy is the ideal to be pursued, unless, of course, it may result in the "wrong" people winning the elections. To this day, Israel and the United States, refuse to recognise the legitimacy of the Hamas electoral victory in Gaza, insisting that they never support "terrorists", ignoring, of course, the occasions when they do. Israel's own "terrorists", such as Menachem Begin and Yitzhak Shamir, were rewarded with becoming the Prime Ministers of that country, despite the fact that they were personally responsible for terrorist outrages. Ariel Sharon is another who was able to operate with impunity despite his decades' long history of anti-Arab violence, with his most infamous involvement being in the Sabra and Chatila massacres in Lebanon. Yet Israel and its leaders have consistently enjoyed the unflinching support of the United States. Not only does Israel receive money, weapons and technology, but it is also regularly safeguarded from reproach by the rest of the world; at least in so far as the rest of the world is represented by the United Nations. The US has unfailingly protected Israel at the United Nations, whether by exercising its power of veto or by other means.

Israel has no questions asked of its nuclear programme and is not a signatory to the Nuclear Non-Proliferation Treaty. According to Israel Shahak in his book *Open Secrets, Israeli Nuclear and Foreign Policies*, "*The development of Israeli nuclear power is financed by the US. Money for this purpose can be obtained only if Congress toes the line of the organized segment of the American Jewish community and of its various allies. And in the process, the American public must be effectively deceived about Israel's strategic aims".* Contrast that with the incessant threats aimed at Iran, which not only has signed the Treaty but can also claim that it does not possess Israel's violent antecedent history, and there appears to be plentiful support for the view that double standards are evident where the West's dealings with the Islamic world are concerned. For example, when considering the consequences of breaching United Nations' resolutions we do not have to look far in order to see the blatant inconsistencies in approach. Iraq was decimated, ostensibly for failing to abide by such resolutions and thereby indicating its scorn for "world opinion", while Israel's disregard for the same institution results in no sanction whatsoever. It is the recipient of more UN resolutions against it than all other countries combined but will never be called to account due to the protection of the United States.

Israel, however, is not the only issue upon which Muslims perceive the operation of double standards. India and Pakistan are two interesting cases in point. Both are nuclear powers but their treatment by the West differs greatly. In more recent times India has begun to exert its economic muscle and is, therefore, understandably courted by the likes of the UK and the US. It was not always thus, however, and yet through-out this period there was a difference in treatment that many Muslims regard as dating back to the days of Empire. Jinnah, the founder of Pakistan, was regarded as the troublemaker for his insistence on the rights of the Muslim minorities, whereas the wily Nehru was regarded much more as "someone we can work with". This perceived bias was viewed as being the reason that, at the time of partition, various Muslim majority areas did not go to Pakistan when, in fact, they should have done under the relevant agreements. The fledgling state almost emerged stillborn as it was also deprived of finance and armaments that again were due to it. Those who regard this as an example of anti-Muslim bias point to the on-going issue of Kashmir as evidence of this. They highlight the fraud by which India sent troops to Kashmir in 1947 as the catalyst for what followed, and observe that despite the United Nations calling for a plebiscite in 1948, this has never taken place. The West since then has called for the independence of other areas such as East Timor (where the occupied are non-Muslim but the occupiers are Muslim), but failed to put pressure on India, despite the fact that the Kashmir dispute continues to destabilize the area.

There is no doubting India's economic power today, and it is understandable, therefore, that this is reflected in the attitude of the West towards it. For decades, however, India's sympathies lay with the communist Soviet Union rather than the United States. It was Pakistan which was pro-American, Pakistan which supported the Afghan mujahideen against Russia on America's behalf, Pakistan which sustained the exodus of Afghans fleeing that war, Pakistan which had to deal with the influx of American weaponry destined for that war and Pakistan which is still paying the price by suffering from the increased extremism which has become the by-product of that war, yet which had played a marginal role in Pakistani society before then. Since then, despite the fact that both countries received censure for their nuclear tests in

1998, (when Pakistan responded to India's tests with a display of its own nuclear muscle), India has been rewarded with a deal for nuclear assistance from the US, while Pakistan's nuclear programme is viewed with some consternation in the West. This may be understandable concern but it fails to take into account the position of Pakistan which is dwarfed by a bigger, more powerful, more prosperous neighbour, which in some quarters still resents the very creation of Pakistan.

Sadly, although Muslims may be justified in pointing out the existence of such double standards in the West's dealing with the Islamic world, they fall into error when they allow this to preclude any proper introspection and self-criticism. It can also lead them to adopt a selective reading of history. Just as many who are ill disposed towards Islam and Muslims choose to focus only on negative examples from the past and present, so, too, do some Muslims ignore aspects of history that do not fit their "West against Islam" thesis. They readily invoke the Crusades but forget that prior to that chapter in history there were significant episodes of mutual trade and interaction, which were not based on hatred. The history of Muslim Spain is a fascinating example of relationships between Muslims, Christians and Jews which were relatively positive and which contributed to the creation of tolerant, thriving cities such as Cordoba. Of course this period came to an end with the Reconquista, but focussing on that, whilst ignoring the previous 800 years, would do a grave injustice to the historical facts. Even the Crusades themselves, showed that a distinction could be drawn between the Eastern

Christians who had learned to live in harmony with others, and their Latin counterparts who clearly had conquest on their minds. Such examples serve to illustrate the dangers of adopting an absolutist approach that relegates great swathes of humanity into one or other supposedly opposing camp.

There is much condemnation by Muslims of the West's military interference in their countries. As we have seen, this can take many forms, from the military and technological support of unsavoury regimes, to the direct military action in Iraq and Afghanistan. Again, such condemnation is often justified, but should not obscure, firstly, other facts of history, and, secondly, military misdeeds committed by Muslims themselves. It can hardly be the Muslim position that we object to non-Muslims exterminating Muslims because we reserve that right to ourselves. There are countless examples of Muslims being killed by Muslims. Some of the most brutal treatment of Palestinians has been at the hands of fellow Muslims. Up to a million people died in the Iran-Iraq War, and perhaps a similar amount in the conflict between West and East Pakistan, which led to the birth of Bangladesh. The Kurds have been oppressed by several Muslim states, while civil war has been a regular feature of certain states in Africa. None of this makes for happy reading and cannot all be blamed on the interference of the West. It may well be the case that the seeds of certain conflicts were sown by colonization, but, although the "colonizer" may have a lot to answer for, questions should also be asked of those who allow themselves to become "colonizable".

The reasons for the weakness of certain Muslim countries is a topic upon which many books can and ought to be written. Suffice it to say that from a Muslim perspective it has to be recognised that we have to get our own house in order first. Yes, Muslims are entitled to, and should, criticise interference by foreign powers in the affairs of Muslim countries, but such interventions are not new. Many Muslims are understandably heartbroken at the devastation wrought, predominantly by America, in Iraq, but even this is not a new phenomenon. When the Mongols invaded Baghdad in the 13th century they were just as destructive in their actions, but the fact remains, that today their descendants are hardly known, whereas Islam and its followers are still a significant presence on the world stage. Muslims should be aware that the idea of one community being "checked" by means of another is referred to in the Quran itself, where God indicates that societies do get replaced by others, and, that this is all part of God's plan, particularly when those societies have abandoned the standards by which they ought to live. First and foremost, being a Muslim should mean living according to certain principles, whether individually or collectively. If they fail in this regard, then they need to recall that Islam is not the property of Arabs, or any other race, and as per the Quranic warning, if they do not live their Islam the way they should, then they will be replaced by those who do.

In attempting to answer questions about the weaknesses of Islamic states one inevitably has to consider the technological deficiencies of certain Muslim countries, which enabled them to be colonized so readily. There were also, however, serious inadequacies in their political organisation, in so far as they were organised, which also played a part in their downfall. Even today we see few examples of Muslim countries where there is a laudable degree of popular participation in the governing of the country, or countries where the level of education is to be envied. As long as politicians in certain Muslim countries think that as their own children will be educated in the West, educating the rest of the nation will only cause them, the leaders, problems in the future, then there is little hope.

There may well be good reasons to resist an American-style democracy, where the ability to raise huge amounts of money is crucial, and, therefore, an almost inevitable recipe for corruption, but the alternative is hardly the despotism that is so often the default position in Muslim states. In fact many Muslims rightly argue that government by "mutual consultation" is a Quranic injunction rather than a mimicking of the West. They suggest that human rights, rather than being a Western invention, actually form the bedrock of Islamic society, yet who would believe this after considering many contemporary Muslim societies, which seem oblivious to the very concept?

Somewhat belatedly perhaps, the focus in parts of the Middle East is shifting from anger directed towards Israel, to anger directed at the deficiencies of their own governments. The issue of the treatment of the Palestinians by Israel remains as important as ever, but there is little disputing the fact that many an Arab regime has used it in the past to deflect criticism of its own shortcomings. As long as it could portray Israel as the source of all the Middle East's problems those advocating domestic reform were never likely to gain much ground. And, more often than not, although there was apparent official enmity directed towards Israel in order to satisfy the domestic population that did not preclude deals being done at state level between these most intractable of foes. The events of early 2011 illustrated, however, that there was an appetite for change among the populations of these Arab countries, and that they did not perceive Israel as the source of all their problems. Similarly the protests were not led or organised by so-called Islamists and few, if any, were seeking refuge behind simplistic slogans like "Islam is the solution". It may be that at the time of writing there is a genuine new dawn for those in the Arab world and that it may herald the start of a new era of useful contribution to the world.

For such a contribution to be authentic it cannot be beholden to Western concerns. In the early stages of the Arab uprisings in early 2011 there was much discussion in the Western media of Islamism filling the void if the despotisms were to be removed. This took little account of the reality that Islamic extremism was playing little or no part in the anti-government demonstrations. Just as this detail appeared to have been missed, or ignored, so too was the fact that although the demonstrations were not "religious" as such, the protesters were not denying their Muslim identity. They were Muslims, they worshipped the One God and were going to continue to practise Islam, it was just that they wanted a say in the way they were governed, and that did not mean they wanted secular tyrannies being replaced by religious ones. This possibility seemed to be totally lost on many western commentators who could not see that perhaps there was an alternative model, which could include religious faith without that meaning rule by clerics.

Contemporary Muslims were showing that they were still angry. Now, however, they were making it clear that their anger was not some randomly directed impotent rage reflecting their stagnation while everybody else passed them by. Rather, it was focussed, considered and fully alive to the opportunities that the modern world had to offer. They wanted to play an active role in that modern world and they wanted to play it whilst remaining committed to their faith.

CHAPTER 6

So who is the Enemy?

I have many fond memories of the 1980s, but, one of my more disconcerting images from that time was seeing, the then Prime Minister, Margaret Thatcher on television announcing after the fall of the Berlin Wall, that, as communism had now been defeated, the next enemy was militant Islam. Excuse me? At the time, militant Muslims may well have been a source of irritation for some, but surely little more, and could hardly be classified as enemies in the same breath as the very communists who had troubled the western world for the best part of half a century. In fact, hadn't they just defeated the very same communists in Afghanistan by virtue of the Mujahideen who were so lauded by the western media? Yes, the very people who later brought you Mullah Omar and his not-so-happy band of Taliban, had heroically seen off the might of the "Evil Empire", having been funded and armed by the forces of freedom. Yet here was one of the very same leaders of the free world teeing up the aforementioned freedom fighters as the next global enemy. The public seemed to be being prepared for the idea that global conflict was not a thing of the past.

It might have seemed somewhat incongruous at the time but it was, in fact, entirely in keeping with the way many Muslims perceived the West as operating. That "way" was perhaps best summed up by events in America immediately following the defeat of communism. Having finally won the Cold War which occupied the decades following the second World War, having lost many lives in that process not only in Vietnam but elsewhere, having conducted wars by proxy across the globe wreaking havoc in the process, and having expended billions of dollars in countering anything vaguely resembling a communist threat, both at home and abroad, one would think that the very next year there would be a reduction in the Defence budget of the United States of America, at least while it gave peace a chance? Not so. The fact that the Defence budget immediately increased just served to emphasize how the USA was seen as being governed; namely by huge business interests, for huge business interests. It also led many to question whether or not communism was really the threat to our individual freedoms as popularly depicted, or whether it was more a threat to a system which pandered to the requirements of the rich and powerful.

The real "threat" was that posed by any system that purported to present an alternative way of life to the unchecked western capitalist model, which so enriched a tiny minority at the expense of the majority. Fortunately for the West, in its communist manifestation, at least, that alternative was seriously flawed and, therefore deeply unattractive to the populations of countries which were understandably proud of their post-war success and liberal freedoms. The images of repression emanating from the Soviet Union clearly made it easier to convince people that this was a way of life which needed to be resisted, especially to Americans for whom God was very much a real presence, yet whose existence was being denied by the atheist forces of communism.

Yet the intentions of the West, particularly of the USA, could be seen in a clearer light when one looked not at their dealings with the Soviet Union, but in their efforts in other parts of the world. It became apparent that it was not godless communism that was being "resisted", but any socially progressive initiative which assisted the poor majority at the expense of the rich minority, and particularly if there was any danger that it may set a good example to others who may want to follow suit. This simply could not be tolerated by the ruling elites, as it would sow the seeds of their own destruction. One does not have to look far to find such instances. The history of US involvement in Latin America is replete with examples of concerted American efforts to undermine genuine democracy if it did not serve the interests of wealthy elites, although of course, these efforts were always clothed in the garb of fighting communism. And the wealthy elites were not necessarily of value in themselves, but more for the capitalist system they supported.

Chile, was a country which had enjoyed over forty years of uninterrupted democracy but with the election of Salvador Allende, in 1970, now had as its president a socialist who was committed to a programme of nationalisation of large industries, as well as insisting on other such unreasonable initiatives as government control of healthcare and education. Clearly this intolerable and the leader of the free world, Richard Nixon, along with his able lieutenant Henry Kissinger, made it his mission to rid Chile of its democratically elected leader, or regime change as it is now known, purely to protect the interests of big multi-nationals, rather than the people of Chile. The CIA was set to work at what it did best, namely, undermining foreign governments and creating instability where none previously existed, and by 1973 an American backed military coup led by General Augusto Pinochet had overthrown Allende and embarked on an economic programme more in keeping with the demands of Washington, than the needs of Chile.

Chile, however, was not an isolated example of American business interests using their lobbying power to influence US policy towards other countries, and, of the CIA being used thereafter to implement such policies, even against democratically elected governments. Countries such as Guatemala may seem relatively insignificant on the global stage but they give a valuable insight into how so-called economic freedom is put into practice, US-style. The political landscape of Guatemala in the early 20th century was dominated by military dictators, backed by the USA. No problem there, even if they were openly fascist, as in the case of one General Jorge Ubico, as long as the policy of granting tax exemptions to American corporations, privatising publicly owned utilities and giving away large tracts of lands remained unimpeded. Inevitably, however, opposition to such rule grew and by the 1940s, following the October Revolution a democratically elected leadership took over. Modest social reforms were implemented but once again these incurred the displeasure of the USA. American corporations such as the United Fruit Company in particular, felt that their interests were being undermined, clearly seeing no apparent unfairness in the methods they had employed in order to secure disproportionate land holdings.

The ensuing election of Jacobo Arbenz in 1950, was due in no small part to his promise of agrarian land reform, undoubtedly good for the people of Guatemala but less so for the likes of United Fruit. The fact that only two per cent of the population owned 70 per cent of the land led the Arbenz administration to enact a law which meant that local agrarian councils could expropriate, and reallocate, uncultivated land that formed part of huge estates, whilst paying compensation to the landowners. As most of United Fruit's land was uncultivated it had a lot to lose. So much so, in fact, that it redoubled its lobbying efforts in Washington to persuade the USA that Guatemala was a Soviet outpost and Arbenz a communist, this despite his inaugural speech promising to make Guatemala a modern capitalist country. What followed thereafter was a US-backed military coup by forces trained by the CIA, the toppling and subsequent exile of Arbenz, and business as usual for United Fruit.

Most of this chapter, indeed this book, could very well be taken up by examples of American efforts to safeguard their business interests in Latin America at the expense of democracy, fairness and the lives of indigenous peoples. Events in relation to Cuba are perhaps the most infamous, particularly with the Bay of Pigs fiasco, again CIA-backed, but it is perhaps easier to list the countries in that part of the world which have remained untouched by Washington's interference. United Fruit, along with others, was also active in Honduras where it again secured tax exemptions and land concessions whilst contributing relatively little to economic growth, not surprisingly perhaps, given that the nation's economic growth was not the reason United Fruit was there, and again the CIA remained involved, particularly as the Contra rebels of Nicaragua were being supported from Honduras by the US. Wherever there were leftist movements, which sought social and economic reform that adversely affected big business, the USA was on hand to undermine them. None of this was new, as the US had consistently supported right-wing regimes favourable to their business interests in Latin America from early in the 20th century.

In Nicaragua, once the CIA-backed dictator Samoza fell, the leftwing Sandinistas took over the government, leading to the CIA supporting the Contras in a guerrilla war against the Sandinistas which later revealed the scandal of illegal arms supplies to the Contras by the CIA during Ronald Reagan's presidency. In El Salvador, Archbishop Oscar Romero was one of a growing group of priests who were now saying that the poor and downtrodden should seek justice in this world, not the next, and had pleaded with the US not to assist El Salvador's military regime carrying out atrocities against its own people. That was enough to get him assassinated and again the odour of CIA involvement has never fully escaped the incident, which became the catalyst for the long and gruesome civil war that was estimated to have accounted for over 60,000 deaths.

In the Dominican Republic the democratically elected Juan Bosch was overthrown by a CIA-backed military coup, replacing him with a right wing military junta. Similar events in the 1960s had replaced Joao Goulart in Brazil, whose heinous crimes included passing a law limiting the amount of profits multinationals could transfer out of the country, nationalizing a subsidiary of ITT and generally promoting economic and social reform. In Ecuador in 1930 President Carlos Julio Arosemena Monroy was overthrown by a military junta after he had criticized the USA and confirmed his support for Cuba. And, occasionally if one of the CIA's own began to step out of line then they too would be dealt with, as the later case of Manuel Noriega clearly illustrated in Panama.

The pattern was a familiar one with the swift and often bloody overthrow of any leader or regime which prioritised the welfare of its people over that of American business interests, and the fact that such regimes were, perhaps inevitably, usually leftist in their outlook meant that it was, more often than not, right wing organisations which attracted American support. Yet, although the aforementioned are merely examples from Central and South America, this should not give the false impression that such efforts to "support" American business were restricted to this area of the world. The reality, sadly, was quite different, with no corner of the globe being spared from the reach of American, and in particular, CIA tentacles.

Even a cursory glance at world events over the last 100 years shows how many regimes have been installed and/or removed at the behest of American business interests. The Western reliance upon oil has led to some particularly disagreeable characters being supported around the world, and, although they have occasionally been removed (or perhaps abandoned is a better description of their demise), it has never happened while they have championed American business interests. From the Shah of Iran to Saddam Hussain, many a despot has been supported as long as he fulfilled his obligations to

America, while democratically elected leaders from Mossadeq in Iran, Sukarno in Indonesia, right through to Chavez more recently in Venezuela, have been consistently undermined by the world's number one democracy, if they dared to have an economic outlook that prioritised anything other than American interests.

The key to understanding this American antagonism is to appreciate that it is not dependent on the colour or creed of the "enemy", but the stance that the enemy has taken towards the way the world economy works. The assumptions upon which that economy is based include that it should be dominated by the West and its institutions. Its leader should, of course, be America and, therefore, American interests come before those of any other country. Naturally, nobody could possibly dispute that such an economy should be based on capitalist principles and that the market (obviously "free") is the proper and just arbiter of how such capitalism is put into practice. Any leader or regime which dared to question such assumptions must be communist and therefore, had to be resisted if the world was to continue to remain free from tyranny.

Now that communism had been defeated and almost immediately replaced by a new enemy in the form of Islam, and the previously anti-communist propaganda was now directing its fire at Islam, there were many Muslims who took the view that perhaps it was not the number of times they prayed that was provoking the wrath of the West, but the fact that their faith may have something to say about how the world economy should operate, and for whose interests.

They began to question to what extent, if at all, Islam was in a position to offer an alternative to the way the world was presently being run, and whether this offered an improvement or not. What could certainly be shown was that Islam certainly had a track record for running a significant portion of the world, and that during that time those countries within its orbit appeared to fare quite well. From Spain in the west, to India in the east, Islam appeared to attract converts quickly, and did not rest at keeping religion private, but rather attempted to ensure that its principles permeated the very running of society. That society, itself, was not without its wealthy people but they too were subject to the rules of the faith and, therefore, had obligations to the poor, which ensured that the gap between rich and poor was never as vast as that which the modern form of capitalism has created. The holy book of the Muslims was certainly not silent on economic issues and the distribution of wealth was a matter of utmost concern to the faithful. Was it possible that it was these features of the religion which presented it as a threat to the economic status quo, and, therefore, to the ruling elites of the modern world.

And, of course, if the above perusal of various Latin American examples is accurate, then it shows that those holding the reins of global power would hardly wait for the alternative society to be created, but would strive ceaselessly to undermine any alternative socio-economic model before it could establish itself and begin to set a good example to others. Present day Muslim countries were hardly setting anything vaguely resembling a good example at the moment but why take the risk of that possibility occurring in the future? Happily, for the champions of unfettered capitalism, many Muslim countries were poor, backward and poorly governed by stereotypically unattractive dictators straight out of Hollywood B movies. All of this made the task of dismissing such countries much easier, but there was always the danger that they may not remain so inherently weak, and, if they ever did get their act together, did they not have a religion which demanded social and economic justice, outlawed usury, and imposed obligations on the rich and powerful? All of this was potentially troublesome and necessitated action on many fronts, not least of which was to constantly undermine the very faith of the Muslims. It was Islam, itself, which had to take the greatest barrage of criticism, in order to ensure it was never seen as an alternative by those who may look for an alternative way of running society.

For this viewpoint to have any credence, however, the presumption upon which it is based, namely, that western society actually needs some kind of alternative approach, must be addressed. After all, is it not possible that those Muslims who hold the above views are not basing them on any inherent flaws in western capitalism, but rather on their own unrealistic utopian vision of a world dominated by Islam? Far from being able to identify any weaknesses in capitalism, a system that they are more than happy to adopt, they just want to have some outward manifestations of Islam, and in the process cause everybody else's life to become correspondingly more difficult. They are simply bitter at their own powerlessness and, for that reason alone, purport to provide an alternative to a system that does not actually need one. They are paranoid in the extreme and see conspiracies where none exist, and rather than simply accept that Western actions against certain

Muslims are justified in order to keep the rest of the world safe, they constantly agitate against the very same West which often provides them with homes.

Recent events, however, may have cast an illuminating light on the above thesis. Even if we put aside for a moment the enthusiasm in certain quarters for the 2003 war in Iraq, and the motives of those who were the loudest cheerleaders for it, are there not plenty of other examples of the West pursuing its interests at the expense of Muslims? The Arab Spring, for instance, was hardly universally welcomed, with the declared justification for the West's reticence being that it would be foolish to welcome a new regime if it was made up of radical Islamists. This argument was, perhaps, super-ficially attractive but ignored the fact that whatever the make-up of the new regimes turned out to be, and there was little evidence to suggest that they were likely to be headed by Islamists, such regimes would inevitably have to do business with other countries, and the basic workings of international politics would mean that extremist edges would have to be smoothed out to ensure the practical success of any new government. This perhaps explains the relatively few extremist Islamic regimes in the world (although, interestingly enough, if the West places Saudi Arabia in this category then it has hardly diluted its support for that particular country). So it may be, after all, that Muslims are right to be wary of the West's approach to Islam.

The recent events to consider, however, do not just involve Western attitudes and actions towards Muslims. Perhaps more importantly, we need to ponder the current state of the West and ask if all is well, or are there serious socio-economic problems that are not indicative of a healthy society. Is there inequality on an unprecedented scale? Has rampant consumerism almost consumed us by degrading our planet so much that our future existence is at stake? Are we, both collectively and individually, having to contend with increasing stresses to a degree, which negates the advantages gained by our ostensibly greater wealth? Despite that wealth, are we in fact, less content and therefore, suffering in our health, both physical and mental, when the material advances of the last few centuries could reasonably have been expected to have guaranteed our improved well-being? Is there greater insecurity and more prospect of conflict? Are we broken, from individual families right through to society at large? And if all this is true, is it symptomatic of a civilisation, which has in fact peaked and, in the future, will end up having to play second fiddle to a strident East? To answer such questions honestly and frankly, one has to consider the ideas and policies of the Western world, as have been starkly brought to our attention during the course of the global economic crisis, to gauge whether or not there are any inherent flaws in the system which make the issue of alternatives an altogether more pressing concern.

It should be noted that the critics of the Western style capitalism that has brought much of the developed world to its knees, are not primarily from the Muslim world. Many an observer has now concluded that the economic convulsions which have wrecked western economies have been due to the shaky foundations upon which such economies are based. Economies which purport to be value-free, in the sense that they simply let the markets prevail (as if this is not a value judgement in itself), are actually heavily laden with values, just not those of the general populace, nor those we expect. Socialism, for example, does exist, but only for the rich, whilst capitalism is reserved for the poor. The whole system appears to have been established, and operated, to serve the interests of the rich and powerful, at the expense of the powerless majority. Debt, both public and private, has reached astronomical levels, where it is now conceded that future generations are likely to be less well off than we are. Advanced societies which thought they had moved on from hardship and want, now see a proliferation in the number of food banks on the one hand, whilst on the other, they are forced to adopt ever-harsher measures in order to placate those who hold the debt. How did we get to this? What makes this economic system work? What are the causes of its failure and what, if anything, can be done about it?

Surely the purpose of a nation's economy should be to serve the general population. Not serve it in the sense of simply providing it with handouts, but serve it by helping create the circumstances in which individuals can thrive on different levels. Man is not simply an economic unit as some would have us believe. There is more to being human than being a cog in a money-making machine. Scientific wonder, artistic genius, emotional connections, all serve to remind us how much more there is to being human than simply being able to generate and spend money. So all a nation's institutions should reflect this truth, and work towards achieving what has often been termed the "greater good", but is erroneously taken to mean the greater economic good. Inevitably this will have an economic aspect to it, but not to the exclusion of other goals and aspirations, and certainly not for the enrichment of a tiny minority at the expense of the majority. Yes, society should cater for the entrepreneurial spirit, without which nations can wither, but it should prioritise the creation of the stability and security that such entrepreneurs need in order to succeed. Do present day western economies help create such conditions or have they been instrumental in putting us in a worse position now, than we were in half a century ago?

When one looks at our modern capitalist economy one is met with an unedifying sight. It is little exaggeration to say that the "city" has become a glorified casino. Gambling, or speculation as it is known on the money markets, has replaced any meaningful and constructive activity, with speculative transactions accounting for over 95% of global daily turnover. Money creation has been passed from governments to private institutions and very few of us seem to realise the dangers inherent in this, failing to see the inevitable conflict between ensuring the well-being of society as a whole, set against trying to maximise profits. Even the way this money is created, literally by the pressing of a key on a computer, has led very few people to question why such "fake" money then has to be repaid by "real" money, once it is loaned out by the very same private banks who created it. These pages will, of course, reveal that I am no economist, but even my simple thought processes can understand how I should repay a debt I owe to another. In the case of the banks, however, it is hardly the case that they take a chunk out of their profits and say "This is our money which we are going to lend to you, so it will need to be paid back". If they did, then clearly one could see the moral and legal case for repaying that debt but, no, they simply "create" money out of thin air, which then appears as figures in my bank account, but then has to be repaid, by real money earned by me. And as Tarek El Diwany astutely asks, why does the state borrow "manufactured" money at interest from banks, when it could simply and legally manufacture it itself, interest-free?

On the subject of money creation, Abraham Lincoln had this to say. *"The government should create, issue and circulate all the currency and credit needed to satisfy the spending power of the government and the buying power of the consumers. The privilege of creating and issuing money is not only the supreme prerogative of government, but it is the government's greatest creative opportunity. By the adoption of these principles, the long-felt want for a uniform medium will be satisfied. The taxpayers will be saved immense sums of interest, discounts and exchanges...money will cease to be the master and become the servant of humanity. Democracy will rise superior to the money power."* President Abraham Lincoln, Senate Document 23, 1865.

This is where we begin to get an insight into the causes of the problem, because when loans from this manufactured money come to be repaid, they invariably have to be repaid with interest. There is, therefore, a very good reason why banks should be happy with such arrangements, and seek to extend them to the most secure of borrowers, namely, western governments. Fake money is created at no cost, in order for it to be loaned out to be repaid by real money, plus a percentage. It is a Mafia-esque racket in which the banks cannot lose, and a situation which is, brazenly but immorally, justified by the disingenuous mantra that we need to repay what we owe; except of course, we end up paying a lot more than we owe, assuming we "owed" it in the first place. This simple system is clothed in convoluted terminology by those who peddle it, in an effort to lend it an air of respectability, but let us just see it for what it is: usury, an economic device prohibited by the world's major faiths, and not without good reason you may think. Not only does it enslave the individual, but entire nations are beholden to it, and because the sums owed keep on increasing, not only will they never be repaid but the cost of even attempting to do so becomes astronomic in terms of the relentless economic growth which is required simply to make the interest repayments. There is then the concomitant effect on the environment as it gets further plundered in the pursuit of the necessary profit, as well as, ultimately, on the communities and individuals who see their lives become worthless during this exercise in tail-chasing.

We are living in an age when public spending is blamed for the economic mess that we are in, so it is public spending that has to be cut, regardless of the fact that it was the reckless gambling and sheer greed of the money men which caused the crisis. Yet the fact remains that if the public debt had not been borrowed from private institutions at interest, the consequences of the debt itself would not have been as severe as they have. Compound interest repayments translate into the following shocking statistics: In 2011, the U.S. federal government paid $454 billion in interest on the federal debt—some 41 per cent of the total $1,100 billion paid in personal income taxes that year. (In the UK for the same period interest payments amounted to some £50 billion with tax revenue estimated to be about £570 billion).

Compound interest in the banking sector increases exponentially and its curve, therefore, begins slowly and then builds into an almost vertical line, which by its very nature shows that it is an unsustainable system. The figures, in our case for public debt, spiral out of control until the whole system is in danger of collapse. To answer El Diwany's question above; if governments borrowed from their own public banks, not only would much be saved on interest payments, and therefore, not have to be taken from the very public services which we all rely upon, but there would also at least be the prospect of repaying the debt, a scenario which is impossible for the modern West.

This debt slavery is not something that is just foisted on the individual. Most of us in the advanced West now readily accept that our lives are not our own, at least not for the quarter of a century or more for which we have signed up to our mortgages. There are those who, perhaps cynically, take the view that this is simply the modern way in which society keeps its populations in check, but it is interesting to note that such tactics are not restricted to individuals but are applied to whole economies. Many a developing world economy has been tethered to the yoke of perpetual debt in a cycle from which it struggles to escape. Yet the very organisations that purport to assist the developing world, are arguably, the ones which only push them further into an indebtedness from which they are unlikely to emerge.

The World Bank and International Monetary Fund sound like respectable organisations whose sole purpose is assisting the less fortunate, yet that is not how they are often perceived in the countries they attempt to assist. They are seen as oppressive Westerners reinforcing a system in which debt is used to control others and money is transferred from public to private hands and ultimately, from poor countries to rich ones. Bodies such as the World Trade Organisation are seen as being responsible for the privatisation of every area of human activity including health, education, water provision and other public services, whilst at the same time safeguarding Western interests in other ways too, such as by supporting the extension of patent laws in ways which disproportionately affect poorer nations.

Titles such as "structural assistance plans" may imply that much economic progress is being made in such countries and, that they are being dragged from their antiquated ways to the prosperity that modernity and reform would inevitably bring, but sadly these titles hide a more sinister strategy. This often involves selling off public assets to private organisations, usually the very multinationals which place profits over the welfare of the domestic populations of those countries. Loans are deliberately promoted to such countries in the full knowledge that they cannot realistically be repaid, thereby justifying more economic interventions such as the purchase of national assets at fire-sale prices, as well as saddling future generations with debt. Thereafter, the same domestic populations lose more of their jobs and public services as draconian measures are implemented in order just to pay the interest on the debts incurred. Any "aid" to such countries in the meantime, is tied up with conditions which effectively sign over their assets to western corporations (often with the usual assistance provided by members of the domestic elite who can be entrusted to ensure that the nation's interest is not the interest that is served).

We see therefore, a system in which only one group wins: the bankers or financiers. Even Mervyn King himself, stated in early 2011 that it was the banks who were to blame for the financial crisis and that he was surprised the public's anger was not greater. His remarks certainly beg the question as to why there has not been any uproar from the masses. Yet the fact remains that despite scandal after scandal, revelation after revelation, it is still the bankers who come out on top, and surely this cannot be down to luck or the superior intellect of individual bankers, but more to a system which is geared for the benefit of the wrong section of society.

At a time when the welfare state is being undermined and portrayed as a haven for scroungers and slackers, it is worth reminding ourselves that the very critics of it seem to have no problem in creating a welfare state for the rich, for that is what we are left with when states ensure that profits are always privatised whereas losses are nationalised. Terms such as "bailouts" seem innocuous enough but what do they actually mean? When normal businesses struggle there is no question of any benevolent party bailing them out, yet despite failure after failure, banks are deemed worthy of such assistance. We are, of course, led to believe that there is no alternative, and we shall return to the question of who it is that helps form and disseminate such opinions, but I have yet to hear a satisfactory explanation for why the money used to bail out the banks could not be used to pay off the deficit.

Despite such obvious socialism (for the rich), we are still fed the line about the free market, a purportedly level playing field where nothing but fair competition determines the winners. This myth conveniently ignores the question of how countries such as the USA achieved their pre-eminence in the world of trade in the first place. Was it by free market rules that they played or did they take full advantage of protectionist measures to ensure their success? Again, what we see is selective socialism, and primarily from the very country where mere mention of that term is anathema to most. The myth also ignores the role of transnational corporations and the fact that the very globalisation which is held up as a unifying force bringing different cultures together, is in fact, a system in which a few hundred corporations control some 65 per cent of international trade, of which 40 per cent occurs between different parts of the same transnational corporation. The extent of their reach in the quest to maximise profits, along with their ability to sniff out low tax environments far and wide, are the only things "global" about them, as the profits tend to accrue in the same old hands, in the same old places.

The market is free, except, of course, when it is not, such as when the state is subsidizing various industries. To take the arms industry as one example, we see how this is an industry which is heavily dependent on taxpayers' money, this merely being one of the ways in which it defies the sacred tenets of capitalism. Now whereas international trade rules ordinarily prevent countries from subsidizing their domestic industries, thereby leading to poor Caribbean countries, for example, being unable to support their domestic fruit growers (which would be so unfair on the rich and powerful countries), we find that by happy coincidence, for the West at least, international trade agreements and the WTO, specifically exclude the military from the rules governing global trade. What this means is that the countries which make the weapons, usually the rich developed nations, are able to subsidize their arms industries in a variety of ways, including purchasing weapons cheaply at home instead of in a normal competitive environment with challengers from outside. The poorer undeveloped nations do not have this option so have to resort to purchasing their weapons from the said rich countries, creating another transfer of wealth from poor to rich. Cynics may suggest this kind of free market perhaps explains why major arms manufacturers such, as Boeing, are all too eager to sponsor meetings such as that of the WTO in 1999, and that it is plain for all to see who is in cahoots with whom, and for what purpose.

This is also an area where we see how relevant value judgements are in the field of economics. Who is it, for example, that decides which industries ought to be subsidized? It is certainly not the case, as free-market proponents would have us believe, that the state does not, and should not, interfere in the workings of the market. Slavery, for example, was a market trading in humans as a commodity, but there came a time when it was felt the state needed to legislate to prevent this happening. More recently, once it was understood that the harm caused by cigarette smoking outweighed any potential benefit, the increase in taxes on, and legislation concerning, this habit effectively influenced the direction in which this market developed. Similarly with the concerns over obesity one can foresee comparable state interventions in relation to unhealthy foods in the future.

In vibrant and robust democracies one would have thought that the domestic populations, rather than just those who wield significant lobbying power, might want some input into these kinds of issues, perhaps preferring it if those industries creating weapons of death and destruction were, in fact, taxed more, whilst any subsidies be reserved for more constructive industries seeking to promote health and the common good. Sadly, the trend, if anything, is for the contrary to happen with decisions increasingly being taken by non-elected bodies, such as the Disputes Panel in the General Agreement on Trade in Services (GATS), conducting closed hearings, yet making decisions which substitute the will and authority of national legislatures.

And through all of this we cannot underestimate the role of the media in selling this flawed system to the masses. It is ultimately from them that we learn that there is no alternative to bailing out the banks. It is from them that we learn to look in disgust upon rioters in 2011, just as we did on miners in the 1980s. It is the media, which acts as the mouthpiece of big business in referring to profits as "jobs", and in failing to highlight the above unsavoury facts about how arms industries operate and exactly what they contribute to the world. Of course, there is the odd piece of investigative journalism, notable by its infrequency nowadays, which may reveal some snippet of corporate malfeasance, but this is portrayed as isolated misconduct rather than as an example of systemic abuse by those who are rich and powerful. It may be, however, that somewhat belatedly, people are beginning to make the connections between the rich and powerful, and the corporate media. They are two faces of the same enterprise, which explains why the increase in corporate power over the last half century has been accompanied by a necessary increase in corporate image-making or public relations, what the rest of us may term as propaganda.

So that is the current system and the suggestion being explored here, is to what extent, if at all, is Islam "under attack" because it has the potential to, at the very least, challenge, and if adopted by a significant proportion of the world, overturn, this prevailing order. We barely need reminding that the Islam being practised by many people today is hardly of the social change variety. It has been argued elsewhere in this book that there needs to be some serious re-thinking on many different levels if Islam is to be relevant to the progress of civilisation, but, for now, what needs to be considered is what, if anything, Islam could *potentially* contribute in the field of economics. Does the Quran restrict itself to the "spiritual" or is it just as keen to address material matters? Is the Quranic prohibition on *ri'ba* or interest, a constructive and viable proposition in the modern world, or simply a commandment that could only operate in more primitive and less sophisticated societies? And as for the recent trend towards "Islamic finance", what exactly does this entail and is it any more than just "Islamifying" the labels attached to conventional banking and finance?

Perhaps the first point to bring to mind when considering any Islamic contribution to society is that it is a way of life, not just an economic theory. What this means, therefore, is that whatever it may have to say about economics, has to be viewed as part of a whole system addressing the concerns of the total human being, not just the economic man. When it addresses the economic concerns of society, these cannot be divorced from its other ethical and moral precepts. To take one example to illustrate this point, Islam stipulates that *zakat* should be payable to the needy by all adult

Muslims who have the means. This is effectively a tax of 2.5 per cent on assets (other than personal assets such as food, clothing and shelter), which have been held continuously for a period of twelve months. As well as promoting a more equitable distribution of wealth, it also serves to encourage a feeling of kinship with one's fellow beings. Also, as it is payable on net wealth, and such assets over time will inevitably diminish in value, it is hoped that it would, therefore, help to stimulate healthy investment and circulation of money, rather than hoarding. It is, in short, just one economic stipulation within Islam applicable to an individual, but it is one that has much wider consequences for the betterment of society as a whole, *if* it is practised properly. That caveat is crucial, however, because if one begrudgingly hands over 2.5 per cent of one's wealth, or thrusts a coin into the hand of a beggar whilst not even being able to afford him a smile, then in all likelihood although the letter of the law would be being followed, the spirit most certainly would not, and in that sense at least, the action could not be described as Islamic, and would not lead to the social change which is envisaged.

So it is that any economic prescriptions applicable to society as a whole, cannot be divorced from the rest of the ethical and moral framework within which we are expected to operate. These include concerns for the environment, for example, as it is central to Islamic belief that all that we have is simply held by us on trust, and one day, we will have to account for how we dealt with it. If, therefore, through sheer greed and wanton consumerism, we set waste to our surroundings and squander our resources, then this in itself would be un-Islamic and something for which we would be accountable in the eyes of God, regardless of whether or not we had paid our 2.5 per cent. Ultimately, that is the goal of all humans according to Muslim belief, namely, that one day we will have to answer to a higher authority for our actions and it is that goal, therefore, which should colour all our actions. It is against such a backdrop, therefore, that we should view what Islam has to say about economic matters and appreciate that its economic solutions, taken in isolation, would amount to nothing more than putting a plaster on a gaping wound, if all its other moral and ethical pronouncements are ignored.

When it comes to economic matters then, perhaps the most well-known of Islamic principles is that it forbids dealing in *ri'ba* or interest. Not only should it not be received, but it should be avoided altogether. The following verses from Surah al-Baqarah (Chapter 2) of the Quran make this clear:

> *"those who devour usury will not stand except as stands one whom the Evil one by his touch has driven to madness. That is because they say 'Trade is like usury', but God has permitted trade and forbidden usury..." (2:275).*

> *"God will deprive usury of all blessing, but will give increase for deeds of charity..."(2:276)*

> *"Oh you who believe! Fear God, and give up what remains of your demand for usury, if you are indeed believers" (2:278).*

> *"if you do not, take notice of war from God and His Messenger. But if you turn back, you shall have your*

capital sums: deal not unjustly, and you shall not be dealt with unjustly" (2:279).

Although these are verses, which clearly deal with usury, they are put into context by the proximity, and message, of the following verses, which emphasise the ethical rationale and moral underpinnings of such rules.

"Those who believe, and do deeds of righteousness, and establish regular prayers and regular charity, will have their reward with their Lord: on them shall be no fear, nor shall they grieve" (2:277).

"If the debtor is in a difficulty, grant him time until it is easy for him to repay. But if you remit it by way of charity, that is best for you if only you knew" (2:280).

That Islam has something to say about interest is understood, but what is less well-known is what other religions have had to say on the subject. The following verses taken from the Old Testament illustrate how the prohibition on usury was also a feature of Judaism.

"If thou lend money to any of My people, even to the poor with thee, thou shalt not be to him as a creditor; neither shall ye lay upon him interest" (Exodus: 22:25).

"And if thy brother be waxen poor, and his means fail with thee; then thou shalt uphold him: as a stranger and a settler shall he live with thee. Take thou no interest of him or increase; but fear thy

God; that thy brother may live with thee. Thou shalt not give him thy money upon interest, nor give him thy victuals for increase" (Leviticus 25:35-37).

"He that putteth not out his money to usury, nor taketh reward against the innocent. He that doeth these things shall never be moved" (Psalm 15:5).

"He withholds his hand from sin and takes no usury" (Ezekiel 18:17).

In Christianity, no less a figure than St Thomas Aquinas argued that usury ought to be forbidden as it amounted to charging twice for something, once for the item itself and once for its use. Perhaps it is not surprising that the monotheistic faiths take this position, but the more one looks into history the more one encounters prohibitions on usury that spanned the length and breadth of the world and its different religions. We find usury condemned by Aristotle and Plato in ancient Greece, condemnation in ancient China as well as Rome, and even early Vedic texts from India and Buddhist scriptures spoke against the charging of interest. This alone should prompt the enquiry as to why there has been this consistent voice against interest throughout the ages.

Yet the prohibition on usury is not a prohibition on trade as is categorically stated in the Quran (see 2:275 above). What is forbidden in Islam is a fixed or predetermined rate of return on financial transactions, not the uncertain rate of return such as that represented by profits. Islam, therefore, stipulates that in order for the investor to share in the profit he must share the risk, i.e. be part of the venture. Simply to invest the money and expect it to be returned with an increase regardless of the success of the venture, would amount to making money simply by having money, and not by taking any risk, or by doing any work or by any effort or sacrifice at all. This making money from money is what is forbidden in Islam and has led to the development of Islamic Banking where the bank is effectively a partner with the debtor. Not unsurprisingly this encourages banks to actively seek out and invest in worthwhile businesses as they have a stake in their success. This can only be healthy for an economy and lead to a more even distribution of wealth, (as well as, of course, avoiding situations such as those which led to the recent sub-prime mortgage debacle).

Islamic banking has become a $300 billion industry and is growing year on year. There is still much debate about how truly "Islamic" some of its institutions and their practices are, but they are still in their infancy and developing. Their growth, if nothing else, reflects a desire on the part of the public for such financial products and it is noteworthy that it is the wider public, and not just Muslims who seek to invest their money in such institutions. If, in fact, they were simply called ethical banks, rather than Islamic banks there would most likely be much less of a stigma attached to them. Certainly their principles appear to be shared by others. The JAK Medlemsbank in Sweden, for example, adopts the following principles: charging interest is inimical to a stable economy; interest causes unemployment, inflation, and environmental destruction; interest moves money from the poor to the rich and favours projects which yield high profits in the short term. Its goal, therefore, is to abolish interest as an economic instrument and to replace it with instruments that are in the best interests of the people, with its main aim being to provide its members with viable, feasible financial instruments, sustainable for the environment and serving the local economy.

It is suggested by some therefore, that despite the deluge of anti-Muslim media coverage, and the appearance of Muslims as some sort of organised enemy plotting to take over the world, this is a deliberately concocted facade designed to obscure the reality, scare the general population, and protect those who truly act like the enemy of the people. They include those who benefit from wars and global instability, those who benefit from arms production and arms sales, those who install and remove regimes to suit their own purposes, and those who help create the cultures that allow all this to take place. Not surprisingly perhaps, behind all such chicanery are those who make money out of it, and more often than not have funded it. They are the ones who economically exploit others and although they wear smart suits and look civilised, there appearance does nothing to alter the fact that they are ultimately responsible for death and destruction on a vast scale. According to UNICEF, 22,000 children die each day due to poverty, at a time when the world of finance is still loathe to change its obscene bonus culture.

In addition, although it may be the economic problems of modern western societies that are the most pressing ones at the moment, it would be foolish to attempt to address them in isolation. They are interwoven with social difficulties. They are interwoven with environmental concerns. Solutions need to be holistic, not just in the way they address the practical difficulties, but also in their appeal to the whole of humanity. Any practical answers need to be part of a moral-ethical framework, which endures beyond the immediate period of unease. And any such solutions need to take account of humanity's spiritual as well as its material needs.

CHAPTER 7

And who are the Silent Majority?

Is there such a thing as normal Muslims? And by normal we do not mean typical because after all, there are more than a billion of us around the planet so it may be difficult to identify what it is that is typical about any of us. It may, in fact, be easier for now to define normal in terms of what we do not mean. So, normal in the sense of not violent, not backward, not enslaved to cultures and traditions that are out-dated, not insistent on oppressing women, not bound to notions of honour which might lead to actions which are contrary to the faith itself, not afraid of, nor hateful towards, those who espouse different beliefs and ways of life, not constantly reminiscing about an idealised bygone age that only exists in our minds, and not averse to using our intellectual abilities to attempt to create a better future for others as well as ourselves. That all seems fairly normal does it not? In short, normal people who have the same desires and goals for their families and communities, as do the rest of humanity.

There are those who would say that of course there are normal Muslims. They would say that such Muslims are the silent majority who quietly go about their business in a law-abiding and civilised fashion. They do not attract or provoke negative reactions either towards their beliefs or their actions, and they live their lives in a way that is in harmony with their neighbours. The fact that such people do not get any media attention does not mean they do not exist. By their very nature they are not likely to seek publicity for what they do, and it is unfair when some negative news item relating to Muslims leads to others pointedly asking "so where is the silent majority then?", the implication being that if such a silent majority truly existed, it would be as readily visible as the extremists whom we see so often and so clearly.

I remember once attending a dinner celebrating the 10th anniversary of a particular firm of solicitors. They happened to be Muslims and it was no surprise, therefore, that many of the guests that night also shared a similar background. Most, therefore, were well-educated British-born Muslim professionals, including those sat at my table. The conversation soon turned to whether Muslims should engage with the media. I was suggesting it was a good idea and expected the rest of the table to agree, and to lament the fact that we were not doing enough of it. On the contrary, however, I was shocked to hear them dismiss the notion out of hand. There was a lack of trust in the media summed up, by the guy sitting next to me, with the line, "a billion of us in the world, and they can't find a positive story?" He seemed to have a point.

Now I have never been comfortable blaming others for the situation that Muslims find themselves in. Undoubtedly others have often had a part to play, and this cannot be overlooked, but it seems contrary to the very essence of Islam, the idea of individual free will and accountability, to then place undue emphasis on the roles played by these others. There are occasions, however, when serious questions do need to be asked about their agenda, especially when this relates to the media. I myself, used to tire of hearing Muslims complain about how the media was so biased against them. This did not mean I had complete trust in the media, far from it, but I just did not welcome conspiratorial theories about hidden agendas, as too often they seemed a convenient mask for our own deficiencies. This outlook was brought into sharp relief, however, by a particular incident that followed on from the publishing of the "Danish cartoons".

These cartoons were deemed offensive towards the Prophet Muhammad by some Muslims, and, some of the more extremist members of the faith, decided that they would safeguard the reputation and dignity of the Beloved Prophet by staging a demonstration in which they donned fake suicide bomber vests and held up banners proclaiming death to the usual suspects. The media lapped this all up and there were headlines everywhere about these undoubtedly fanatical protesters, as well as images of the hideous banners they displayed. This gave a particularly negative impression of Muslims, particularly as there was a gross distortion in portraying the demonstration as significant in number, when, in reality, there were less than a hundred such protesters.

Yet in the very same days that this particular news item was being aired, I happened to be at my mother's house on one occasion, when she was watching one of the Muslim satellite channels. This channel was beaming live pictures from Trafalgar Square, London, where there was another type of demonstration taking place. This time there were tens of thousands of British Muslims who had packed out the square. This time the banners being held aloft read, "Thank you Britain for not publishing the cartoons".

Regardless of the rights and wrongs of the publication of the cartoons, surely the question was this: what would the effect of the Trafalgar Square images have been on the British public? One can reasonably conclude that they would have been given a valuable, conciliatory, and constructive insight into the "silent majority", but sadly these images were nowhere to be seen on mainstream news channels, nor did they merit any mention, let alone headlines, in the press. Had those images from Trafalgar Square been shown to the general public, in all like-lihood they would have had a positive effect on the public's perception of Muslims. They would have been able to put into perspective the actions of the extre-mist minority when viewed against the backdrop of the peaceful majority. The fact that the peaceful demonstration took place in the heart of London meant that there was no excuse for not knowing about it. It seems reasonable to assume, therefore, that conscious decisions were made not to show such positive images and it is appropriate to question why. In not showing such images, any debate about the existence and role of the silent majority of Muslims is prevented from properly taking place, with any discussion being restricted to the usual topic of extremism. This, in turn, reinforces the view of many that there exists a specific agenda in maintaining a particular aspect of Islam in the forefront of the public's mind, to the exclusion of other facets of the faith and its followers.

The media's responsibility needs to be highlighted as it is instrumental in forming opinion about the silent majority, but it has an, arguably, limited impact on the reality of the group itself. Who are the "normal" Muslims and what is it that they do? Who speaks for them? Is it enough for Muslims to be normal in the sense of being law-abiding members of society, or should they be doing more? Are there differing strands of thought available to Muslims or do they belong to a monolithic bloc, which allows for no divergence of opinion? Is Islam set in stone or is there room for debate and dissenting views?

Most people, reasonably conversant with current affairs and regardless of their faith backgrounds, are nowadays aware of some of the basics of Islamic belief and practice. For example, many of us are aware that Muslims pray five times a day, they fast in the month of Ramadan, and they go on pilgrimage to Mecca. These are established duties enjoined upon Muslims, but do Muslims, themselves, ponder these practices, or are they simply content to follow the established rituals? Are they even allowed to ponder on these practices? These are some of the questions to be examined here and the answers will assist us in considering whether or not Islam is simply a relic left over from an era of religiosity, or whether it can still have relevance, and perhaps more importantly, any use in the future.

The Quran was revealed at a particular time, the early sixth century, in a particular place, desert Arabia, to a particular people, the Arabs. Yet its message is said to be applicable for all of mankind throughout the ages. Can it remain relevant and applicable without any human input, or do we have a responsibility to keep it relevant, and if so, how? There are many examples where this debate can find fertile ground but the following perhaps illustrate the point clearly. One of the pillars of Islam is that Muslims should pray the five daily prayers. The times for these are roughly as follows: dawn, midday, mid-afternoon, sunset, late evening. It makes sense to look at the rationale behind these timings and conclude that they are an attempt to instil in the Muslim (literally, he or she who submits to God), the desire to remember God constantly, by marking out certain parts of the day as times to put our worldly concerns aside, and put worship first. When we consider the context in which the rules regarding prayer were revealed, we find, unsurprisingly, that Arabia in the sixth century was a society, which measured time by reference to the sun. The working day was effectively governed by daylight hours and the prayer times reflected that.

Things have moved on in the last fifteen centuries or so. Despite the wishes of many people, Muslims are not confined to the Middle East, but now inhabit practically every region of the world, including Scandinavian countries where, in Norway, for example, the north of the country has days in the winter months when there is no daylight at all, and, conversely, days in summer where there is no darkness. What should Muslims do there? Neither omitting prayers completely, nor praying continuously, appear attractive or viable options. Fatawa (legal opinions) from religious "scholars" have emerged, therefore, permitting the following of the nearest Muslim country on the question of prayer times, but these appear arbitrary and inadequate as solutions, and not necessarily in keeping with the spirit of the original requirement to pray. Does Islam really prevent the adoption of an alternative, which is consistent with the spirit of the injunction and yet practical in its application?

In the United Kingdom in the winter months the last four daily prayers can be as close as 12 noon, 2pm, and 3.40pm, with the final prayer being at 5.30pm, hardly the end of the day. Yet the same final prayer ('Isha) takes place as late as 11pm in the summer months. The dawn prayer is at 7am in winter but a somewhat inconvenient, and therefore more readily missable, 3am in summer. Is this what God intended? If the requirement to pray according to the position of the sun is unalterable, then one could argue that it is. If however, the sun timings were simply revealed because that is how the recipients of the revelation happened to measure time, then we can see the theoretical possibility of alternatives being made available to the Muslim community. Also, rather than any verse stipulating the inherent holiness of the sun and moon, we actually find the opposite. There are Quranic verses (such as 6:96) clarifying that the sun and moon are not inherently holy but relevant for the purposes of marking time.

Now in the modern world very few of us mark time by reference to the sun. The vast majority of the developed world's population tells the time by referring to their watches, not by looking out of the window. Recalling that the purpose of the five daily prayers appears to be marking the day so as to remember our Creator at regular intervals, what is there that should prevent us from adopting the following timetable, in Britain for example: Early morning prayer at 6am, midday prayer at 12noon, afternoon prayer at 4pm, early evening prayer at 7pm and late evening prayer at 10pm. These times could apply throughout the year. There would be certainty with a single prayer time applying throughout the country unlike the present situation. The day would be divided up with times allocated to the worship of God, times which are more consistent with the nature of the working day in many modern societies, and with such certainty employers are also likely to be more amenable to their workers taking time out for their worship. Of course there can be fine-tuning according to the requirements of different countries, and in-built flexibility and allowances where exceptions need to be made, but none of this appears to contravene the spirit of the faith. On the contrary it keeps the faith meaningful and relevant in the 21st century.

It would also have an added advantage for another pillar of Islam, namely, fasting in the month of Ramadan. The Islamic calendar is based on the lunar year so we find that Ramadan does not always fall at the same time, and is generally about ten days earlier each year. At present in the United Kingdom, for example, when Ramadan falls in the winter months the daily fast is roughly from 7am to 4pm. Yet in the summer months, it can be as long as from 3am to 10pm. Now let us for a moment consider the purpose of fasting. It is clearly stated in the Quran that fasting is prescribed to us so that we may "learn self-restraint". It is also made clear in the Quran that our Creator does not seek to put us in any "hardship". Now, going without a spot of lunch in the winter months is, arguably, not going to teach us a great deal of self-restraint. Similarly, going without food and water for up to 19 hours in the summer months, as well as the loss of sleep involved in getting up for the 3am breakfast and prayers, could arguably be described as hardship, and, is perhaps going to make us feel more tired and irritable, rather than closer to God and spiritual.

Again it is useful to bear in mind that when God told the Arabs in the sixth century to fast from dawn until dusk he was giving them a fast which was more or less consistent with their working day. As it happens, the position of Arabic countries in relation to the Equator means that the length of the day there is roughly the same in winter as it is in summer, around about 12 hours. So God was telling the Arabs to fast for about 12 hours, and such a fast would be entirely feasible if one adopted the revised prayer timetable suggested above, namely, starting the fast with the early morning prayer at 6am, and ending it with the early evening prayer at about 7pm. This would not only be consistent with the working day but would also allow for the reflection and prayer which should be part of Ramadan, but, which is a struggle in the summer months when the night prayers only end shortly before the next fast begins, leaving little time for any reflection or contemplation, and would thereby satisfy both our spiritual and material needs.

There is yet another "pillar" of Islam which could arguably be re-considered. (It is perhaps understandable, if somewhat unfortunate, that these tenets of the faith are described as pillars as it gives the impression that perhaps they are intended to be immovable, when, in fact, the label is a man-made one rather than God-given.) The Hajj, or pilgrimage to Mecca, is a duty on all adult Muslims, to be performed at least once in their lifetime. A lesser, voluntary pilgrimage called the Umrah, can be performed at any time of the year but the Hajj itself must be performed at a particular time. Every year, despite the best efforts of the authorities, the sheer logistical nightmare of administering up to 2 million people in one place can cause all sorts of crowd control problems, presenting physical dangers to the pilgrims. Is this what was intended when the Hajj was first made obligatory?

Now that there are a billion Muslims in the world, what if they were all to turn up on the same day to perform their religious duty? In doing so they would merely be attempting to fulfil their religious obligations, but would be prevented by the authorities from doing so. Practical reasons, involving the safety of the general public being placed ahead of religious duties, would mean that accommodations would be made which would be deemed not to contravene the spirit of the religious requirement. Similarly we see how many of the rituals that form part of the Hajj have, themselves, been modified, again in order to meet human needs, rather than any perceived Divine ones. The symbolic stoning of the pillars, representing the shunning of evil, is now the stoning of large walls with basins underneath to catch the stones and avoid accidents. Routes are made one-way to avoid the dangers of trampling tragedies. The sacred Hajr e Aswad, or Black Stone, does not have to be directly touched but can merely be pointed towards, such is the sheer volume of people attempting to approach it.

The fact is that such accommodations are already being made in certain areas and therefore, at least theoretically can be made in others. It is not difficult, for example, to envisage a time when there are so many Muslims wishing to perform the pilgrimage that it is simply not feasible to have it occur on one day in the year.

Could we then have a scenario where the authorities say that the Muslim population has now reached such a size that in future the Umrah will count as the Hajj? It could, therefore, be spread across the year taking away the logistical problems and the attendant safety issues. And if, as some suggest, the purpose behind the Hajj is to create a meeting place where Muslim issues and problems can be addressed, a sort of annual conference, then is this not likely to be more useful if it is attended by those who are in positions of authority and leadership. An annual convention where Muslims bring not only their problems and grievances, but also their ideas and solutions, is probably long overdue and, arguably, some way off into the future given the current state of the Muslim world, but it is the type of progressive initiative which the community is crying out for.

The point being made here is that there is scope for religious rituals to be amended to suit changing circumstances and such amendments are not contrary to the faith, but, as is so often the case, they tend to only become unobjectionable once established. Innate religious conservatism makes this tweaking of tradition anathema to many followers of the faith so the impetus for such change cannot come from lay people but scholars, thinkers and those with a measure of authority in Islamic matters. It should also be emphasised that these are ideas held by, or at least articulated by, just a small minority of the Muslim population, but, it is suggested nevertheless, that they are ideas which need to be considered if Islam is to remain relevant to the modern world. It needs to be clarified that they are not ideas contrary to the spirit of Islam and are only contrary to the letter of the law if one takes a literal approach to it which not only goes against its spirit, but can also, on occasion defy common sense. These are the kinds of ideas that need to be addressed by the religious authorities of Islam if they want to avoid being marginalised and want to avoid their faith becoming a collection of meaningless rituals. It is normal in other faiths to tackle questions of tradition versus modernity; resistance to change versus progressive evolution of religious practices and it should become the norm in Islam too, rather than the preserve of a tiny reform-minded academic elite. These are the topics that Muslims should be discussing over dinner.

So, what is the normal kind of thinking going on in the Muslim world? Is there any thinking going on in the Muslim world? In attempting to gain some insight into the views of normal Muslims perhaps the most useful starting point is to listen to some of the voices of Muslims themselves. We are all too familiar with the inflammatory ranting of various extremist preachers but, given their very limited following, they clearly do not appear to represent the majority of the community. There are no significant protests at their detention, for example, and one can well understand that most Muslims would gladly see the back of them and be able to concentrate on their own lives and families. Yet these preachers almost appear to have a tacit understanding with the media whereby they manage to get their desired publicity, and the media their stories, regardless of what most Muslims may actually want. Just so as we are clear, it is accepted that the media have a right and duty to inform the public of the existence of such extremists in our midst who, at the very least, have derogatory things to say about our way of life, and may well impact on our security. Any objection is simply to a disproportionate and distorted representation that neglects the existence of other voices.

It is useful, however, to look at some of the other representatives of the Muslim faith, particularly those who have the advantage of being highlighted by the media. Firstly we shall consider those who are critical of Islam and Muslims, bearing in mind that such criticism comes in a variety of forms. It must be conceded that it is not easy to assess just how representative such voices are. Book sales would be somewhat indicative if it were not for the fact that they do not necessarily denote approval. And of course the way such publications are marketed undoubtedly has an impact on the sales figures in any event. Three, quite diverse, authors who are often held up as being powerful critical voices, if only for the reason that each comes from a Muslim background, are Ayaan Hirsi Ali, Irshad Manji and Ed Husain.

Perhaps the easiest to deal with is Ali who sets her stall out clearly. Having been born in Somalia, later renouncing Islam and ultimately finding love in the arms of an American neo-conservative, she is, unsurprisingly, not the Muslims' first choice when it comes to self-criticism. She was undoubtedly subjected to ill-treatment in her early life, which the offenders purported to justify in the name of Islam, but the conclusions she draws about the faith, rather than those responsible for the ill-treatment, show a lack of understanding of Islam which detracts from her value as a critic. Being born into a faith does not necessarily confer understanding, although that is not to demean her experiences. Sadly she has become little more than a neo-con poster girl, content to be the stick with which they can beat Islam.

A more interesting critic is Irshad Manji. Her Canadian background perhaps made escape less of an issue for her than for Ali, but she too was subjected to ill-treatment, this time by a knife-wielding father. Although at first blush one may again question the objectivity of any criticism, which is set against such a backdrop, her work merits serious consideration. Her background in the media may explain her penchant for shock-jock tactics and these, coupled with her being openly lesbian, will be enough to send many Muslims running. My first reading of her book, *"The Trouble With Islam Today"*, left me similarly nonplussed, as her constant bleating about being on the verge of leaving Islam made me want to shout back "Just bloody go will ya! Sort it out with God because quite frankly I can't be a**ed." Her tone seemed to evince a barely concealed contempt for Islam and Muslims and that was the abiding impression left with me. It was the kind of book that I really had to take a deep breath to pick up, rather like tuning in to another depressing episode of *Eastenders*. You knew it was going to stress you out, and life was difficult enough without this self-inflicted dose of further angst, so why put yourself through it? Well, not only did I put myself through it, but after a suitable period of recuperation, I decided to go back for a second dose. The question was whether or not it was just her style that I found objectionable, or were there, in fact, issues with the substance of her work?

Manji should undoubtedly be given credit where it is due. It is difficult to argue against her calls for honesty on the part of Muslims. She is absolutely correct when she asserts that too many Muslims have developed a victim mentality and are voluntarily keeping themselves in ignorance, faults which they need to get rid of urgently if they are to contribute usefully to the modern world. When she states that certain Arabs have been setting Islam's agenda for too long, she probably has a point worthy of further investigation. Her three proposals for progress, namely, "revitalising Muslim economies by engaging the talents of women; second, to give the desert a run for its money by unleashing varied interpretations of Islam; and third, working with the West, not against it", are utterly commendable. But, regrettably, the six-line paragraph which contains these proposals is obscured by the overwhelming weight of negativity, indeed contempt, which she comes across as displaying towards Islam and Muslims, and it was the latter which stayed with me, a second time reader who actually had some sympathy for her views.

I cannot help but think that to a large extent her attitude is coloured by her personal experiences. She is to be congratulated, however, because it was recognising this very trait that encouraged me to think that if her negative experiences could inspire her to write about Islam, then, perhaps, so too should my positive experiences similarly motivate me. Not only does her work reveal her family difficulties, but, also, that the environment around her did nothing to draw her towards Islam, rather, in fact it distanced her further. Many Muslims growing up in the West will feel similarly about their flawed communities, but the difficulty of course, is that it results in Manji having no love for the Muslim community, and her calls for reform, therefore sound more like those of a condescending outsider rather than a mournful insider. As any parent will know, rebuking and admonishing has its place, but ultimately there needs to be a degree of sympathy and mutual understanding for true change to take effect in the hearts you seek to influence.

That sympathy is singularly absent in Manji's approach to Muslims who never receive the benefit of any doubt that she may have. She insists on drawing conclusions adverse to Muslims and such is her wilful refusal to acknowledge evidence that may justify a sympathetic conclusion, that the prospects of reaching some mutual understanding recede further with every turn of the page. Her very description of Islam as being a "gift of the Jews", betrays a completely flawed understanding of what Islam means and where it stands in relation to other faiths.(It does, however, perhaps explain what she later has to say about Israel.) She says that she desires reform but the very Muslims who would be expected to form the vanguard of such reformers, are alienated further when she insists on showing not the least respect for the Prophet Muhammad, a man they are taught to love. For example, her description of the killing of the men of the Jewish Banu Qurayzah tribe is reduced to a simple command to "kill the Jews", leaving the impression that this must be some sort of Muslim duty if it was ordered by the Prophet himself, and that it involved killing them simply for being Jews. One would have thought she may have at least considered the account given by Karen Armstrong in her biography "*Muhammad*", which puts into context the treatment of convicted traitors in the seventh century, particularly when they brought a community close to extermination, and highlights how the punishment was, in fact, one chosen by an arbitrator nominated by the Qurayzah themselves. Manji is entitled to come to whichever conclusions she thinks appropriate but to disregard certain arguments because they do not favour her agenda will inevitably lead to readers questioning her motives.

A similarly fast and loose approach to the facts is evident from her treatment of the Quran. If her work is an honest and genuine call for reform then surely the holy book of the Muslims demands serious consideration. Manji, I believe rightly, criticises those who do not adopt a contextual reading of scripture, yet she is more than willing herself, to pluck verses out of the book that suit the particular point she is attempting to make, without addressing their context, stating that it is unclear which verses were revealed when. Again, that assertion may carry more force if it was based on some serious study of the origins of the text. Not once does she admit to the difficulties inherent in analysing a text simply through a translation, yet without doing so she resembles the Japanese student of English literature who, having read a Japanese translation of Shakespeare, wonders what all the fuss is about. To speculate that "it's conceivable that the compilation of the Quran had to be rushed to meet imperial pressures", might be a weightier proposition if it was not just based on an article in *"The Atlantic Monthly"*, and took into account the fact that although the compilation of the written document might have been treated in a particular way, it was nevertheless the case that many people had already committed the Quran to memory by that stage.

But perhaps most importantly of all, in this "wake-up call for honesty and change", why not include, indeed promote, the many interpreters of the Quran who are modern and educated, reformist and progressive, and unlike her, have bothered to address the original language of the book, yet do not feel the need to question its authenticity, at least not on spurious bases? These are the voices that need to be heard if Islam is to contribute usefully to the world, yet ignoring them only gives the impression that they do not exist. Abdullah Saeed's *"Interpreting the Quran"* is an excellent introduction to analysis of the Quran, and in particular, a contextual reading of it, and deserves at least a mention in Manji's work. Tariq Ramadan, Reza Aslan and others are notable by their absence. And as for the many eminent female Muslim scholars and interpreters of the Quran why ignore them, unless of course, they may disagree with you? Amina Wadud's seminal work, *Quran and Woman*, sadly finds no place in Manji's rant.

Manji is equally dismissive of Muslim history. For her it seems like it was nothing but the incubation period for all the ills of the present day Muslim world. Muslims ruled and/or were a significant presence in Spain for some eight centuries, yet this deserves barely a mention, despite the fact that it helped create the flourishing "ornament of the world" in the city that was Cordoba. The House of Wisdom established at Baghdad merits fleeting attention, despite the fact that it attracted the greatest minds of the time. The Muslim presence and continued influence in Sicily is now being belatedly recognised as playing a instrumental role in the European Renaissance (see inter alia John Hobson's *"The Eastern Origins of Western Civilisation"*) yet does not get Manji's juices flowing. Sadly she can only find "wholesale discrimination" where others find a degree of civilisation that was unmatched in the rest of the contemporary world. Lest it be thought otherwise, I have argued elsewhere that Muslims cannot rest on the laurels of previous success but, if Manji is seeking to promote a new climate of thinking amongst Muslims, then surely emphasising, rather than demeaning, the Golden Age of Islamic history is vital.

In Manji's glass-is-half-empty kind of world the only relevant fact of Muslim history, and one that seems to require emphasis and repetition is the "Pact of Umar". Now I would like to think that I am reasonably clued up when it comes to Islam. As will be apparent by now I am certainly no scholar, but I have read a bit and am certainly familiar with the major formative events of Islamic history. Yet I have to confess that the first time I came across this Pact was in Manji's book. This event that she describes as having a "decisive effect on early Islam – and beyond", was one that I had never heard of. Well, of course, that is hardly the criterion by which to judge its authenticity but, doing a little research, I discovered that there certainly was considerable doubt about whether this document could properly be attributed to Umar, the second caliph of Islam, or Umar II of the eighth century. No matter, what did this document, whose authorship was in dispute, actually have to say? According to Manji, "It decreed that non-Muslims shall stand when a Muslim wishes to sit, that non-Muslims shall watch their houses of worship decay without repairing or replacing them, that a Muslim's testimony in court shall trump a non-Muslim's". Pretty grim reading without doubt, but not edicts which sit comfortably with the Covenant of Umar, the second caliph of Islam, made with the Patriarch of Jerusalem which stated, *"This is an assurance of peace and protection given by the servant of Allah, Umar, Commander of the Believers, to the people of Jerusalem. He gives them an assurance of protection for their lives, property, church and crosses, as well as the sick and healthy and all its religious community. Their churches shall not be occupied, demolished or taken away, wholly or in part. None of their crosses nor property shall be seized. They shall not be coerced in their religion nor shall any of them be injured."*

Manji expressed surprise at how the "Pact of Umar" was associated with the second caliph, whom she described as, a "decent and thoughtful fellow by almost every account I've read". All of which begs the question why highlight a document of dubious origin when it does not accord with what you do know of a significant and respected figure of Islamic history? And despite asserting that all the notes and sources for her contentions can be found on her website, I could find there nothing of note to substantiate the authenticity, or indeed purported impact on Islamic history of this "pact". To me this was another example, and a doubtful one at that, of Manji insisting on including an anecdote or interpretation that was unfavourable to Islam and Muslims. There is nary a mention about what conditions were like at that time for other religious minorities. The general acceptance that the Muslims were relatively better in their treatment of others is conveniently masked behind the fact that they had the temerity to impose a *jizya*, or tax on their non-Muslim subjects. This is quoted as an example of Muslim discrimination without clarifying that the tax exempted the non-Muslims from military duty. In other words, they could claim the benefit of state protection without the concomitant obligation to fight for that Muslim state. And the conclusion of all of this cursory research on the part of Manji enables her to "grasp how Islam has come to be an insular, often hateful religion." There is no such thing as a "self-hating Muslim" but if there was such a label, Manji would be vying for the title.

So far, this "wake-up call for honesty and change" has questioned one of the most fundamental Muslim beliefs, namely the divine origin of the Quran, but has done so without any compelling evidence other than the fact Manji struggled to make sense of it all. She has gone on to question the very character of the Prophet, again refusing to give him the benefit of any doubt, when often his worst enemies would struggle to say anything against him personally. Islamic history apparently contains little or nothing of use to humanity. Perhaps understandably, with her attack now in full flow, it seems that her inclusion of Israel into the list of complaints about Muslims was intended merely to administer the coup de grâce. Fair enough she did get a paid trip to the Holy Land and it would be downright rude to criticise them after their hospitality, particularly as it seems the Palestinians were not as keen to fund such a trip, but there does not seem to be even the semblance of any objectivity about the Israel-Palestine dispute. It may well be right that this should not be the defining issue for Muslims seeking to live their lives in the West in the 21st century, but there should surely be an acknowledgment of the victims of the dispute. Countless United Nations' resolutions against Israel might just indicate what most of the world thinks of the rights and wrongs of this dispute but Miss Manji's bile-fuelled juggernaut is not for slowing down, let alone stopping.

The Israel-Palestine problem is not the simplistic one that many Muslims might think and Manji is correct to state that the issue has been exploited by some within the Muslim world. However, she is not content to stop there because for her, once again, the main blame lies with the Muslims. Muslim extremism is bad but Jewish extremism is fine. She seems oblivious to the fanatical rants of the likes of Rabbi Ovadia Yosef, (voted the 23rd greatest Israeli of all time in a poll by the Israeli news website *YNet* in 2005, the year Miss Manji's book was published), who is responsible for such gems as "Gentiles were born only to serve us. Without that, they have no place in the world – only to serve the People of Israel". Her view of Israel is through such a distorted lens that she goes so far as to say that Israel, in fact, implements an affirmative action policy towards its Arab citizens. One wonders then why so many Jewish writers are critical of Israel if such benevolence is its hallmark, rather than, for example, the discriminatory Law of Return. She is content to quote as an "eminent scholar" the historian Bernard Lewis, which would be unobjectionable if she perhaps balanced his views with those of writers such as Noam Chomsky, Norman Finkelstein, Amos Oz or numerous other eminent Jewish scholars, who incur the wrath of the pro-Israel lobby by being deeply critical of the state of Israel.

Dear Irshad Manji, many of your criticisms of Muslim individuals and states are perfectly valid, and if the truth be told, perhaps long overdue. But please help me with this. I appreciate that controversy sells, and the spectre of one Muslim putting the boot into her co-religionists is undoubtedly going to boost your readership, but amongst whom? Yes I know you have many supporters, but at what cost? How many Muslims have you alienated with your distorted take on Islam and its adherents? Having not spared the Quran, the Prophet Muhammad, and Islamic history, you then insist on topping it all off with some, I would say, frankly unnecessary, cheerleading for Israel (I mean is that really the cornerstone of any Islamic reform?). So what is there that is left for reform? I know that ideally you would want an Islam that is consistent with your world view but I really do not think that is what it is meant to be about. I am the first to agree that there needs to be fresh interpretation of much of what has passed as Islamic in the past, but where was your discussion of the inherent spirituality and system of ethics that Muslims need to rediscover if they are to make Islam the force for good that it once was, and ought to be again? Then again, I suppose you do not think it ever was, which may explain why your passing references to anything half-decent in the Muslim world are buried under the overall weight of condemnation and contempt. I sincerely hope that I am in a minority of Muslims who are put off by your approach because there is no doubt that Muslims need to do some serious thinking/re-thinking, and in so far as your work assists in that regard, you have my support.

Ed Husain, on the other hand, finds me less sympathetic. Ed, Ed, Ed. Why on earth, for a start, would you want to abbreviate Mohamed to Ed? Ok, I accept it is a matter for you, and maybe again your research showed that books by Eds outsell those by Mohameds, at least in the West, but do you not think that many Muslims might be put off by your new nom de guerre? After all, you know how sensitive some of "us" are. I have allowed myself to be sidetracked, however, because I, for one, am not particularly offended by your choice of name. No, I am afraid my concerns lie elsewhere. *"The Islamist"* is very readable and, to be fair, it does make some very pertinent observations. You will have to forgive me, however, if I don't buy this "inside track to radical Islam" approach which suggests the reader is about to unearth some grave and hidden secrets about the workings of various shady organisations. To be perfectly frank, many of us, and by us, I mean those who were never extremist nutters in the first place, find that your book simply confirms what we suspected all along, that those who veered towards extremism were those who, like yourself, were "never quite settled", "a loner at school, occasionally bullied and frequently sworn at", "a misfit" with "no white friends" who suddenly "felt very special" when they joined what they thought was this Global Rude-Boy Massive which was given a righteous air by virtue of its "Islamic" credentials.

I may be being unfair because like I said there are some useful observations in your book and I genuinely hope it has steered some impressionable youngsters like yourself away from radicalisation. On the other hand, however, there are those who feel you are simply one of those guys who bends whichever way the wind blows, and, because anti-radicalisation is flavour of the month (not to mention where the funding lies), that is the explanation for your "conversion". I am not so sure. I do believe that you are genuinely "moderate" now, and have a greater insight into Islam. But my goodness it took an inordinately long time for the penny to drop for you. I mean what on earth were you thinking, a grown man, working in the City, studying at university, realising that your Islamist ways were a mistake, and then after 9/11 asking "how are we going to celebrate?" Really? You were not sixteen years old then, and I'm afraid the "hold" you claim Islamism had on you escapes me.

I think a lot of educated Muslims want to believe you but have some serious reservations regarding your credibility. You will be very familiar with the term "sell-out", and it is an easy one to hurl in your direction when there are those who simply think you are saying what your paymasters want to hear. I do not necessarily think, however, that it is accurate in your case, but you sure make it difficult for those of us who want to defend you. I mean there are not many Muslim organisations you have spared in your accusations and this in turn may be counter-productive. After all, surely you want to have as many Muslims as possible on board with your sentiments about "true" Islam, so why seek to alienate those who hold some degree of authority with Muslim communities? That is not to say that they are above criticism but surely a more diplomatic approach would be more fruitful. I know your background is one of seeking confrontation but one of the advantages of growing up is that we can see the futility of tactics that seemed attractive when we were teenagers. The alternative is that more often than not people wish to dissociate themselves from you, which is sad because much of what you purport to believe now is what Muslims, in fact, need to think about.

Another example of your diplomatically ham-fisted approach is your Quilliam Foundation, or Quilliam as it is now known, named after the 19th century English solicitor William Henry Quilliam, who converted to Islam and, having taken the name Abdullah, thereafter headed up a Muslim community which was quite progressive in much of its outlook. What you clearly did not appreciate, or bother to look in to, was the fact that in Liverpool, the birthplace of Quilliam, existed the Abdullah Quilliam

Society which, for several years, had been negotiating with the local council to obtain and refurbish the old site of Quilliam's mosque to transform it into a modern heritage centre. This would firstly preserve a significant part of British history, a building which many consider to be the first independent mosque in Britain, and secondly, be a base from which to educate people that Islam is not an immigrant religion brought over just by Pakistanis and Arabs, undoubtedly highly pertinent when it comes to pressing issues of social cohesion as I am sure you would agree. In its efforts the Abdullah Quilliam Society works in conjunction with, and with the full support of, Quilliam's remaining descendants. Did you bother to ask the family if you could use their name? Did you make contact with the Society and inform them of your intentions? Sadly you did not, which made the Society's efforts much more difficult when it had to spend an inordinate amount of time and energy distancing itself from the Quilliam Foundation once you became mired in controversy.

And controversial you are. Let us ignore for the moment the fact that you proceeded without any regard for the above Society or the wishes of Quilliam's family. Let us also put to one side the suggestions that you are in bed with the government, particularly the former New Labour one, and are furthering their agenda at the expense of the Muslim community. Let us consider another example, a documentary in which your sidekick Majid Nawaz went to Pakistan on some anti-radicalisation drive. Cynics would suggest that certain organisations have to justify their existence and/or funding, and therefore make a bit of a show of their efforts. I have no problem with that and well understand your enthusiasm to take along a film crew. There was a telling moment in the documentary, however, where Nawaz was at a university in Pakistan talking to some students. He was explaining the evils of radicalisation, which is fair enough, although these were educated youngsters he was patronising Ed, not ignorant villagers, when one of the students said something along the lines of "That's all very well and we agree, but what do you say about the Iraq war?" A clearly embarrassed Nawaz was left mumbling some inane response! I mean is this what it has come to Ed? You self-confessed bad-boys of Islamism who sought and revelled in confrontation, are now rendered speechless because you are in the pay of the State? Where does that approach leave your credibility and how can you seriously persuade Muslims to join your "reformist" efforts when they are queuing up to distance themselves from you?

Happily for Muslims, those who advocate fresh and independent thinking in Islam are not restricted to the Manjis and Husains of this world. In so far as their efforts are sincere I truly hope they get a reward that is commensurate with the publicity they undoubtedly have received, but there are others out there who do not attract such publicity but whose efforts nevertheless, are noteworthy.

Muslims need to rediscover the spirit of constant intellectual renewal which played such a significant role in their history, but is notable by its absence in recent times. To some extent that was understandable given upheavals caused by the period of colonisation, but this explanation only goes so far. It can no longer be used in an age when colonisation has ended, and education and learning is so readily available to much of the world. Having said that, it would be a mistake to suggest that there is little or no thinking going on in the Muslim world. Tariq Ramadan is perhaps the most prominent intellectual to raise issues of reform but he is not the only one. Reza Aslan is one of the new breed of Muslim hero, fearlessly tackling Islamophobia on the one hand, and outdated rituals on the other, doing all of this in a readily understandable Western idiom. Amina Wadud has grappled with the controversy of a female interpretation of the Quran, despite being the object of opposition by many in the world of traditional Islamic scholarship. Her work *Inside the Gender Jihad* addresses the issue of women and reform in Islam, a subject about which one would think there was no mention by any Muslim, let alone by a female scholar of Islam. Khalid Abou el Fadl brings reason and tolerance to the fore with his extensive knowledge of the Holy Scriptures as well as Islamic history.

The fact remains that such thinking does not necessarily get the publicity it merits. Even when reform-minded efforts need every ounce of support that they can get, we find that opportunities are spurned. One such advocate of reform in his book *"Islam, Liberty and Development"* said the following: *"The effect of dogma on our society, which has a religious identity, is vast. And its negative effect is greater than secularism because dogmatic believers usually project an aura of religious legitimacy...Centuries of our history have been governed not by the conscientious and thoughtful effort of the people of the land, but by autocratic and whimsical rulers...Freedom of thought, which represents the key condition of being present on the stage of destiny and the main impetus for dynamism and growth in social life, has not been respected in our society...Our temperament has not been trained to be receptive to freedom...In the past half-century, every time the ground has been ripe for us to experience freedom, we have squandered the opportunity.*" Sometimes such sentiments emerge from directions we least expect. In this instance, these words were penned by Mohammad Khatami, the president of Iran from 1997–2005.

They are just a few names but, happily, the efforts are not just those of individuals. Countries such as Malaysia and Turkey have long been involved in reformist thought, and Turkey's recent announcement that it was going to undertake a long-term project which aims to re-interpret the scriptures in the light of contemporary knowledge, is welcome even if long overdue. Their efforts were not ones of political expedience intended to satisfy the West, but were an authentic initiative from within Islam which involved extensive work by the School of Theology at Ankara University, precisely the kind of focussed and practical scholarship which the Muslim world had been missing for so long. Such efforts are not only necessary, but also give hope that the future for Islam need not be as bleak as many of today's headlines may suggest.

CHAPTER 8

How Is it looking for the future then?

I grew up on a diet of chips. No, I do not mean the greasy potato pieces, which are regarded as "traditional" English cuisine, nor am I referring to the potato based snacks eaten by our American friends but which, we, having invented the language, quite properly call crisps. No, I am talking about "*CHiPs*", an American TV series about the California Highway Patrol. Its stars were Jon, a very plain waspish blonde American, and his sidekick Ponch, the exotically named and equally exotic looking Frank Poncherello, who, perhaps coincidentally looked like a Pakistani bloke. They were two motorbike cops who patrolled the Californian highways and saved the day on a regular basis, well, every Saturday on ITV at about 5pm, to be more precise. *ChiPs*, along with *Starsky and Hutch*, *Dukes of Hazzard*, *Knight Rider* and later *Miami Vice*, were the shows that provided the heroes for many a kid in the late '70s and early '80s, my formative years, and along with equally glossy soaps such as *Dallas* and *Dynasty*, gave this youngster a portal to a world where everyone seemed bronzed and beautiful, a glamorous glossy world which, to a youngster born in Burnley, was how he pictured heaven might look. Never mind the 70 odd virgins that the tabloids thought I was promised, I was just happy if heaven was going to be full of Pamela Ewings and Daisy Dukes.

So why do you need to know this? Because it gives an insight into what it was that I found most appealing growing up. In fact, to this day I can recall clearly leaving the cinema with a pal of mine after watching *Beverley Hills Cop* in early 1985, with both of us vowing to relocate to California. Needless to say, neither of us did move there, and are both still in Liverpool, but back then it just did not get any better than the USA. That, therefore, hopefully sets the scene for my later criticism of certain aspects of American life or, more particularly, its foreign policies. Such criticism is not based on some inherent hatred of all things American which is supposedly drilled into Muslim children from an early age, but is the result of years of witnessing certain actions which were, firstly, worthy of condemnation, and secondly, all the more upsetting because they began to dismantle the idealised picture of America that I had grown up with. Of course, it is one thing to see a place on TV but surely the reality would not be as exciting and attractive. Yet when I paid my first visit to New York in 1990, shortly after graduating, I still found it to be a place that, like many of the products sold on its streets, gave you an incredible buzz and got you hooked.

(It was also my first trip abroad and I learned the invaluable lesson that if you are a dark skinned chap with a goatee beard, you do not run through an airport in New York. My flight had been delayed considerably and I was mindful that Andrew, with whom I was going to stay in

New York, had been waiting for some time, so as soon as I picked up my luggage I began to run, well jog, towards the exit. Unfortunately, there was a huge queue there. Fortunately, as I joined the back of it, a helpful looking police officer approached and asked me to accompany him. As he took me towards the front of the queue I distinctly remember thinking "Oh man, how cool is this? The guy has seen that I've only got one bag and am in a hurry, and figured there's no point in me wasting time in the queue so he's helping me bypass it. Only in America!" Imagine my surprise then when he then took me to one side and asked me to open my case. Fortunately, he only found my clean underwear and other accoutrements of the first time traveller. Unfortunately, that did not allay his suspicions and he went off and returned with a tiny screwdriver with which he began to prod in search of a secret compartment in the case. It was at that point that I remembered that the suitcase belonged to my grandfather and had been brought by him from Pakistan, so for all I knew it probably did have a bloody secret compartment! Just as I began to contemplate life in a small cell with a big man, the officer begrudgingly sent me on my way.)

To this day, however, my criticism of America is equalled by my admiration and attraction for it. Now that I am grown up and happily married, obviously I spend less time thinking about Daisy Duke or her modern equivalents, but I am still impressed with American achievements, particularly in film and music. That is not intended to be some sort of backhanded compliment, because I can readily accept that, over the years, perhaps there have been a few American achievements in areas other than entertainment. I am firmly of the view, however, that the quality of some of America's creative output is second to none and provides an unexpectedly thoughtful analysis of modern society, whether that be at home or abroad. Films like *Syriana*, *Body of Lies*, *Lions for Lambs* and *Rendition* are admirable for their willingness to explore themes that may be uncomfortable for those who regard American conduct as unimpeachable. TV series such as *The West Wing* are not just products of genius written by people at the very top of their game, but also provide a commentary on what America is and what it could be. (How many of us have secretly wished that the President of the USA really was Jed Bartlett, or even Martin Sheen himself for that matter, seeing as acting seems to be a necessary quality in that particular office?)

Perhaps this discussion of American entertainment does nothing more that highlight one important fact. I am not, nor do I want those around me to be, interested in just holding one-dimensional views when approaching world affairs. America is not simply either good or evil, and although much is made of it being regarded as the "Great Satan" by certain parts of the Muslim world, so too, do Muslims suffer from being equally poorly and prejudicially regarded by sections of the western world. America should certainly be taken to task for its misdeeds and, perhaps it can be argued, that from those to whom much is granted, much will be expected and, in the context of America, this places on it a greater responsibility to ensure that its stability and prosperity are used for the greater good rather than merely to enforce its own interests around the world. This may be regarded as a utopian ideal but if we are to progress beyond our current materialist obsessions, then someone somewhere is going to have to take the lead. But, at the same time, just because I may on occasion be critical of America, does not mean I blindly support every act committed by those calling themselves Muslims, whether they are acts committed individually or collectively, and in this approach, I firmly believe that I am supported by my faith which exhorts me to forbid evil and enjoin good, no matter which "side" it may be coming from.

Unfortunately, some Muslims have fallen into the trap, whereby they all too easily overlook the crimes committed by their own, and, instead, focus on those of others. One of the regrettable side effects of this is that it contributes to the creation of the victim mentality with which so many Muslims are afflicted, and, which, over time reduces the effectiveness and dynamism of a community. To me, this is against the very essence of Islam, which makes it abundantly clear that part of the bargain for our free will, is the responsibility that comes with it. By blaming others for our misfortunes, we are shirking our responsibilities and ignoring the Quran itself where it is said;

> *"God has promised to those among you who believe, and work righteous deeds, that He will of a surety grant them in the land, inheritance (of power), as He granted it to those before them; that He will establish in authority their religion (deen), the one which He has chosen for them; and that He will change (their state), after the fear in which they (lived), to one of security and peace" (24:55).*

This appears to be a promise in the clearest terms. Worldly power, security, peace and the prevailing of their way of life, is promised to those who "believe and work righteous deeds". Muslims need to ask themselves who it is that possesses these benefits in the world, and why. There appears to be no room in the above verse for blaming others, but rather the plainest of exhortations that if you do the work then you will get the reward. That, of course, does not absolve others of blame when they wrong you, but your responsibility lies with those matters within your control.

So, how we live our lives is crucial to our success not only in the Hereafter, but also here on earth, as the above verse makes abundantly clear, and, how we live our lives will be influenced in no small part by the values according to which we operate. Whether we admit to it or not, we all live by certain values. Even if we choose to deny any ethical or moral imperative in life, then that, in itself is an assertion of the values by which we have chosen to live. In each generation no doubt, issues will arise which lead us to assert or question our values. The evil that had to be confronted in the form of Hitler, for example, was an assertion of our value system in the last century. More recently the way we have reacted to the MPs' expenses scandals and the overweening greed of bankers shows that there is still something within the human psyche that objects to such conduct.

It may just be that such objections are more difficult to bring to the surface in societies which place over them as many insulating layers as we seem to do now. Materialism, in its various forms, muffles the very sound of those objections. The western world has enjoyed unprecedented levels of prosperity in recent times, which has served to dull our senses and increase our apathy. It is little exaggeration to suggest that modern western societies have been created in which we are encouraged to become addicted, and consequently, distracted. Whether it be illicit drugs or legal ones, football or reality television, we are bombarded with inane, meaningless activity which further removes us from those things that should matter, and as long as we get our regular fix of these opiates, we can see out our lives in relative contentment. Perhaps those who compare these distractions with the gladiatorial contests, and other sports, of Imperial Rome have a point, given the decline that seems to be facing the West now.

The question arises, therefore, as to where our values should come from. Ironically the proposal here, that religion, certainly in the form of Islam, offers us a solution, has, itself, had to endure being regarded as an opiate. This accusation, regrettably, is not without foundation because it cannot be denied that there are those who have used it to control the masses. History has many examples of those who have imposed religion on others for political ends, but often even those who have chosen to adopt religion of their own free will, have all too readily conceded their autonomy as human beings. They may well have held genuine and sincere beliefs but they have too frequently allowed others, supposedly more religiously qualified or knowledgeable, to speak for them, and, perhaps more worryingly, think for them too. In recent times we have seen at close quarters the direction that this can lead a minority of extremist followers. They can be the cause of much damage to society, but that is nothing as compared to the damage they inflict on the religion that they purport to follow. This valid criticism of religion as an opiate, however, should not mask the fact that other ways of life can also be used to control the masses in a similar fashion. How often, for example, have we seen all manner of crimes being committed in the name of democracy, with the very invoking of that word expected to stifle any criticism right from the outset.

The danger, therefore, is not in religion itself, any more than it is in any other way of life, but rather is in the abdication of personal responsibility in both thought and deed. Islam, contrary to the views of many of its critics, certainly does not advocate such an abdication of personal responsibility. It is, of course, central to this faith that humans are ultimately accountable before their Creator, but this does not mean that every sphere of human life is, or should be, governed by so-called "religious" rules. Many Muslims, themselves, are bliss-fully unaware that for many centuries Muslim scholars were not afraid to question even the most fundamental beliefs and practices stipulated by Islam, yet nowa-days even the slightest deviation from the perceived orthodoxy is met with accusations of blasphemy and infidelity.

It is no coincidence, however, that the era of debate and dissension coincided with periods when Muslims had military and material strength and, more important-ly, the psychological security that that brought with it. Now, when many Muslims feel under attack and there-fore assume a siege mentality, they become unnecessarily defensive and retreat to the perceived safety of orthodoxy. Everything becomes either black or white because, with all the uncertainty around them, the grappling with new cultures and languages, the military superiority of other nations, the educational shortcomings of many Muslim nations and the incessant negative media coverage of all things Islamic, the one area they regard as a safe haven is their faith. Others may well criticise it, or sadly even ridicule it, but for Muslims, there is the reassurance of something firmly rooted in a world that is changing at an ever-increasing rate.

This is precisely the area, however, where Muslims have to wake up and realise exactly what it is that they have turned Islam into, and what, in fact, it should be. Is it just a system of comforting rituals, which really does act as an opiate, taking away the pain of the real world? Or, is it, in fact, a way of life that urges constant endeavour and action to improve ourselves individually and collectively, tackling problems rather than shying away from them, all the while remembering that ultimately we are answerable to the Almighty? A way of life which recognises that there is more to life than just the physical and material components that we can empirically assess, yet, a way of life that is holistic and does not compartmentalise the physical and the spiritual, but accepts rather that both should play a role in creating the successful individual, and thereby, society. And, if this is what Islam should be, can it be so without any active involvement on the part of its followers? Is it a ready-made mix, which requires no further input from believers but simply has to be applied like an ointment over our wounds, or is there a role, and a significant one at that, for Muslims themselves?

There is nothing wrong with the Muslim belief that the Islamic way of life should emanate from the guidance provided to humanity by God Himself. The Quran is where we should look for this guidance, whilst bearing in mind that we are more than just passive recipients of this revelation. It is not by accident that we have been endowed with the most complex and powerful of faculties in the shape of our brain, the full capabilities of which we still do not completely understand. It does not make sense, therefore, that we would be given this powerful tool if all that we are expected to do is to passively receive the guidance and implement it without any thought processes of our own. Furthermore, is it perhaps rational to think that maybe one reason we have been given such capable brains, is because the problems facing us as human beings, do not remain the same but constantly change, and, therefore, require new and innovative solutions? We have the intellectual capacity to come up with those solutions but, being human, when left to our own devices we also have the ability to come up with creations which are more harmful than beneficial to society and therefore, we are very much in need of guidance. It is entirely reasonable to conclude that such guidance is best coming from an objective, external source, one that is familiar with our workings and knows what is best for us, despite ourselves.

The Quran provides that guidance but it is interesting to note that it is not The Million Commandments, when of course it could have been. It is believed by Muslims to be the direct word of God, revealed over the course of 23 years to the Prophet Muhammad, through the angel Gabriel. Now if God had so desired, it was entirely possible for him to simply dictate commandment after commandment, and no doubt, in the course of almost a quarter of a century, He could have dictated a fair few. Yet, He did not. The Quran is not the ultimate rule-book. It contains many similes and parables. Much of it is allegorical. It covers specific contemporaneous instances as well as general examples from history. Many of its themes are repeated. This to the outsider, especially one not familiar with the language or cultural idiom involved, often leads to the erroneous conclusion that it is a bit of a muddle which has extensively borrowed from other religions. Such conclusions are amateurish and do not take account of the basic requirement of the Quran, namely, that it requires its reader to think. Time and again it instructs us to ponder our surroundings. Not only does this help us to understand its similes, its historical and scientific examples, and, thereby, its Divine authorship, but it should also lead us to reflect on why it is that the Quran is not simply a rulebook.

We need to be able to distinguish between the values of our faith, and individual laws that apply for a particular time and place but can be modified in due course if the requirements of society so dictate, as long as the underlying value system is adhered to. There are those Muslims, for example, who insist that music is forbidden in Islam. I do not believe that it is, as there is certainly no verse to that effect in the Quran. More importantly, however, the question should be asked as to what Islamic value it offends against, and here we find that the discussion becomes more nuanced. Militant rap music advocating violence and the sexual objectifying of women clearly offends against several Islamic values, so one can appreciate any argument suggesting it ought to be shunned. But it is difficult for me to accept that all forms of music, even the most exquisite of classical pieces, are forbidden according to my faith. As it happens, I love listening to music. It can be inspirational and uplifting, or simply relaxing and enjoyable. It clearly brings joy to my children, who seem to share my eclectic musical taste, which includes everything from Guns n Roses to Sami

Yusuf, The Elgins to The Prodigy. (In fact, there was a time when my son would happily wander round the house singing along to Frank Sinatra's Love and Marriage, although he would always sing "hope and marriage", and had to be constantly reminded by me that there was no hope!) How could I, therefore, insist on an interpretation of Islam that excluded such a beautiful part of life. There is a tradition of the Prophet stating that "God is beautiful, and loves beauty", so we need to think long and hard before legislating prohibitively.

We also need to remember that even such laws as there are in Islam, are not an end in themselves. The laws, the religious rules, the behaviour deemed desirable, are all intended to assist us on our path towards God, our ultimate destination or return, and the mere observance of such is of little use if it does not help us on that journey. Islam is not supposed to be a religion for box-tickers. It is supposed to be the blueprint for the "civilizing mission" which is what humanity is all about. Constant endeavour so that the human race is always improving is what religion should inspire us to do, yet often, our behaviour suggests we are going backwards. It is sometimes regarded as a liberal sign of enlightenment and progress when music and films contain more expletives than they used to in the past, when women wear less and less in the name of choice, and when life is generally characterised by fewer inhibitions. Yet the logical conclusion of this trend is that it leads us back to where we started: naked and coarse like the cavemen we once were. Progress indeed. We need to consider which direction we should be moving in, individually and collectively, and consider which social constructs assist us in that regard, and which hinder us.

We have created a multitude of rules for ourselves as Muslims. There are "rules" for every aspect of life including sitting down, standing up, walking, talking, and every type of action and interaction that it is humanly possible to achieve. There are different categories of edicts from the mandatory, through the desirable, to the voluntary. Yet next to none of these emanate from the Quran itself. There are of course, secondary sources of scripture where certain of these "rules" can be found but the basic commandment is quite simply this: heed the Quran. When we do as we are thus instructed, we find a book which does not have rules for every last detail of life, but, in fact gives general guidance. Indeed, often the general principles themselves are not readily apparent, but have to be ascertained as the result of a process of reflection. This in turn, cannot be achieved without an understanding of the context in which the relevant verses were revealed. One has to have an understanding of the circumstances prevailing at the time, in order to fully appreciate what exactly is meant by certain verses, which appear to contain specific commands. In short, anybody seeking to properly understand the Quran has to accept that some effort will have to be made, but also be open to the fact that such effort is well within the capabilities with which we have been endowed. Life should be about constant positive human effort and in this regard it is bound to be the case that such positive effort will also reap its rewards in our understanding of the Quran.

It is suggested here that this very process of applying ourselves to a contextual analysis of the Quran leads us to a position from which we can hope to derive the general principles that we can apply to our modern lives. We can ascertain what have been described as the

"Divine objectives", and see how they were imple-mented at the time of the revelation, but then we also need to consider the needs of our own societies today. It is certainly not an intrinsic part of Islam that all the rules which were applied in 7th century Arabia are pertinent and relevant to 21st century Britain, or America or even any modern Muslim state for that matter. Those who think that the "Shariah" is some system of laws that is set in stone, never to be changed, are mistaken as to the meaning of the word, and the very concept it denotes. In order to be able to effectively legislate in accordance with Islam, we have to under-stand the needs that have to be legislated for, or in other words, understand our societies, and this, in itself, requires us to develop anthropological studies and sciences which inform us about society. One cannot legislate in the field of genetic engineering, for example, by just having recourse to the scriptures and no knowledge of the science in issue. In adopting this considered approach we begin, therefore, to take the first tentative steps to making Islam relevant for our society, rather than being a relic of the past concerning itself solely with ritual worship.

There is an important Quranic lesson that illuminates this point. The prohibition on alcohol is a famous Islamic "rule", yet the way in which it came to be prohibited is highly instructive. There are three significant verses relating to alcohol in the Quran. The first in time states that in alcohol (and gambling), there is some good and some harm, but that the harm outweighs the good. The second relevant verse exhorts people not to come to the mosques whilst intoxicated, this clearly having been something that the Arabs at the time were not averse to doing. The third verse states to avoid alcohol altogether. Now it cannot be denied that it was well within the power of the Almighty to simply announce in the first revelation that alcohol was forbidden, but He did not, and it is incumbent upon us to question why. The only sensible explanation is that the society was simply not ready for that prohibition, so, rather than issue a commandment that would simply get ignored, the Almighty, in His infinite wisdom, prepared that society for the eventual demise of this habit. "Prohibition" is exactly the right word as it brings to mind that period of American history when alcohol was unsuccessfully prohibited for a society, which was not ready or willing to desist from its consumption. Contrast that to the banning of cigarette smoking in many public places in the West in recent years. Not a blanket prohibition, but the first steps on a course, which ultimately persuades and prepares society to accept for itself, that cigarette smoking is to be avoided. Then when at some stage in the future a law might be passed "prohibiting" it, society's view of it will have evolved enough for it to more readily accept such a law.

This type of approach to Islam is advocated by many so-called reformists and here we find another area fraught with difficulty. "Reform" has become a dirty word to many Muslims. I recall a few years ago attending a lecture by Tariq Ramadan on the topic of Reformation in Islam. Outside the building I was met by some very smart young Muslims who were handing out various leaflets. I assumed they were part of his young, educated following and they were handing me some information about the lecture. I was somewhat shocked to discover, therefore, that the leaflets were along the lines of Islam does not need any Reformation. Yet, what exactly do we mean by reform? The above suggested approach to the Quran, and the way we should legislate for our society, is arguably little more than common sense, yet the fact that it may attract the ire of many Muslims does nothing more than highlight the stagnation in our thinking. Any type of change is condemned without thinking through exactly what it is that is being found objectionable. Scholars such as Ramadan who are straining every synapse to consider how Islam should remain relevant for our society, are condemned by those who regard thinking as being optional. Such people deploy a conservatism which may help them cope with the demands of modern society, but they fail to realise what they leave behind in their wake. Their own children end up either just going through the motions of religion, or adopting ultra conservative and insular positions which do them no service in today's world, or simply abandoning their faith. Non-Muslims look at Islam from the outside and see nothing they regard as of use to their lives and think that this is a faith which, if anything, discourages free thinking. Ultimately, the very idea of reform in Islam is left to a select group of academics whilst the rest of the community carries on regardless.

This has to change. It may be that people view the word "reform" itself as objectionable. Fine. Find another word. The word does not matter but what is of crucial importance is the approach it purports to advocate, namely thinking about one's faith. Not through the eyes of Arabs in the 7th century, but through contemporary eyes which are assisted with the latest knowledge about their environment. Muslims need to have at the forefront of their minds the constant Quranic reminders to reflect, and use their powers of reason, and if this is done sincerely and determinedly, then there is hope for the future of Islam. Also, this is not an approach, which is the sole preserve of academics. The likes of the Ed Hussains of the world and their Quilliam organisations which have lost their credibility with so many Muslims, need to be shown that the followers of the faith can think for themselves and do not need organisations deemed to be "sellouts" to lead the way. Those like Irshad Manji should be shown that Muslims are not the stereotypical backwards caricatures that she invokes, and do not need to be insulted and have the very foundations of their faith undermined in order for them to keep that faith relevant today. Those who are used as neo-con cheerleaders such as Ayaan Hersi Ali will naturally fall by the wayside if a new movement for thinking in Islam captures the imagination of Muslims.

None of this can be achieved without the firm foundations provided by an education. This means both for men and women! How much longer can Muslims in some parts of the world continue to try to justify wilfully ignoring half of their community's talents, abilities and ideas? If a woman is man's equal in the eyes of God, which she certainly is according to the Quran, is it not reasonable to expect that she ought to be his equal when viewed through his own eyes. The answer is obvious, even if in some quarters it is long overdue. Too many Muslims, particularly men, have failed to take advantage of the educational facilities available to them, especially in the West, and for this failure they will one day have to account. Not only have they squandered opportunities for themselves and their families, but they have also done a great disservice to their faith. They have placed themselves in a position from which they struggle to distinguish their religion from their inherited cultural baggage. And if they are not clear themselves, how can they criticise others who, mistakenly, but understandably, confuse honour killings, forced marriages, female genital mutilation and other culturally driven social deficiencies, with Islam, i.e. submission to the Creator? The sad fact is that too few of us have an understanding of Islam beyond following a few of its rules.

One of the areas in which a lack of education impacts negatively on Muslims, is their susceptibility to being "played", or their gullibility. It has almost become a sick joke that if you want to get Muslims to start rioting and end up killing each other, then all you have to do is press their buttons. Say something offensive about their Prophet and then leave the rest to them. The very Prophet who patiently bore insult after insult, would probably be turning in his grave at the thought of what certain Muslims were doing in the name of safeguarding his "dignity". There is little doubt that the absence of useful knowledge and critical understanding certainly plays its part in the mindless riots, which are orchestrated in certain parts of the world whenever such "offences" come to light. The organisers often have their own ulterior motives for these demonstrations of religious objection, but the fact that their populations have little in the way of education leaves them open to be manipulated.

Such manipulation comes in many guises. There are those who are ill-disposed towards Islam and Muslims and exploit certain sensitivities about matters deemed to be sacred, and then there are certain leaders in Muslim countries who manipulate their populations' indignation at, for example, perceived offences caused by non-Muslims. The conclusion that even the most enlightened of Muslims now reach, however, is that the media plays the most significant part in exacerbating the problem, knowing full well that there is a ready ear for hearing negative stories about Muslims. Thus it is that a vicious cycle develops in which negative media reporting creates anti-Muslim sentiment, which is then fed by further negative media reporting. The result is an atmosphere so pernicious that rational thinking is jettisoned and heels are dug into respective positions. When the usual stereotypes are highlighted, the collective mood of the nation has by now become so moulded by these opinion makers, that people look no further than the obvious explanations. The result is that in an age when it is media sound-bites that prevail rather than proper analysis, we show that we have learned nothing from the history of the last century, and are more than content to sit back and watch one particular community become the scapegoat.

The seeds of the later (and justifiable) complaints of rational Muslims were, in part, sown in the '70s and '80s with the subconscious racism and anti-Muslim sentiment which was created by seemingly innocuous, action B-movies from Hollywood (such as the prodigious output of messrs Menahem Golan and Yoram Globus) which invariably portrayed Muslims or Arabs as terrorists or useless playboy millionaires. It is precisely that kind of culture, which helps to form a nation's psyche, so that subsequently, when it becomes expedient to point the finger at a particular group, society is ready to accept unquestioningly that group's guilt. The examples of those convicted of grooming young girls for sexual exploitation in England was highly instructive, with certain sections of the media emphasizing the religion of the offenders as if, firstly, it played any part in their offending, and secondly, as if they were typical examples of their faith communities. But as this particular dog had already been given a bad name, its subsequent ill-treatment was going to raise little in the way of objection. It is another tawdry episode relating to Muslims, whom we have been taught by now, have no redeeming features, either individually or collectively. The fears and insecurities of non-Muslims are being exposed on the one hand, and thereafter fuelled by the amplification of the misdeeds of certain Muslims on the other. Any hope of inter-community harmony is thereby extinguished as people are separated into rival camps. This "divide and rule" tactic works on so many levels, leaving the powers that be to continue their privileged rule whilst the masses are preoccupied with fighting each other.

A particularly illuminating example of how society can be moulded to ask no questions when it is the "usual suspects" who are being blamed, is that of "Revolution Muslim" in the United States. It is the kind of story that you would struggle to make up, but, as ever, truth proves stranger than fiction. The creators of *South Park*, the American cartoon series, decided that they would depict the Prophet Muhammad on the 200th episode of their show. It was nothing particularly offensive but that did not stop a radical group known as "Revolution Muslim", based in New York, from issuing threats against the *South Park* creators, suggesting that their actions would result in their untimely deaths. No surprises there you may think, given how mad Muslims obviously are. Not surprisingly CNN picked up the story, and sadly, no surprises either, when CNN decided to give the story much publicity, implying thereby, that this group was somehow representative of Muslim views. So far, so predictable, but this is where things began to get interesting.

The founder of the radical group was one Yousef al-Khattab, but his real name was Joseph Cohen. He was born and raised in the United States as a Jew, and held both American and Israeli citizenship. In the late eighties, Cohen embraced an ultra-orthodox inter- pretation of Judaism, and began attending a yeshiva (rabbinical school). In 1998, Cohen like many American Zionist Jews before him, packed his bags in order to relocate to the Israeli Occupied Territories where he became an Israeli settler. As an ardent and extreme Zionist, Joseph Cohen fell in with the Jewish funda- mentalist group *Shas*, an extreme right-wing political party. Yet, less than three years later, Cohen had "converted" to Islam, having had some online chat with a radical Muslim cleric whom, having clearly worked his magic on this particular Zionist, you might think would have used his powers of persuasion on the rest of Israel and promptly solved the Middle East conflict with just his trusty webcam, but alas not.

Cohen/al-Khattab, thereafter moved back to the United States, and founded the most radical Islamic group in the country. This is, as far as I am aware, the first time such a committed Zionist has switched to radical Islam but of course, that in itself, does not mean it is not true. Anyway, together with his sidekick Younus Muhammad, a similarly mysterious "convert" to Islam from extreme Zionism, they formed "Revolution Muslim" and then, despite their conversion to a new faith, began to adopt an agenda, which could only have been authored by somebody with a real hatred of Islam. For example, one of them claimed that the Quran commands terrorism, conveniently just the type of comment that a hard-core Islamophobe would want to announce to the world. Considering the founder's background in an extreme right-wing and funda- mentalist Israeli political party, Muslims have every reason to be suspicious. Although on any view, "Revolution Muslim" was just too convenient, that did not stop the media from portraying those two "Muslims" as being representative of millions of Muslim Americans. Cohen/al-Khattab was giving the mainstream media the narrative they wanted to hear, namely, that Muslims, violent and irrational as they are, simply lose their minds when the Prophet Muhammad is depicted, and this was a message that society had, by then, been well-prepared to receive.

The example of "Revolution Muslim" is an extreme one which makes the point emphatically but there are plenty of instances of more subtle games being played with an all too gullible Muslim community. For the last few years Sufism has been a much-discussed topic in the western world but the circumstances of this discussion do give some cause for concern. To many Muslims, Sufism represents the mystical or spiritual essence of their faith, what they would regard as the reality, the substance of faith, rather than the mere form represented by outward obedience. It is regarded as properly understood and practiced by those who are devout and sincere, and have more than a passing acquaintance with Islam. To some, however, it is seen as a rejection of all worldly matters and a retreat into a more spiritual place.

This essentially is a debate that exists in other faiths too, the tension between form and substance, the material and spiritual, and one can appreciate that it is a debate, which is properly addressed by only the more deep thinking of individuals. Yet during the currency of the anti-extremism drive in post 7/7 Britain, it became quite a popular topic of discussion.

Now it may have been that it was an entirely sincere discussion and I was being just another unduly suspicious and paranoid Muslim, but I was somewhat surprised at the increasing number of times that I was being asked about whether or not I was from the Sufi branch of Islam. My answer usually began with a slightly surprised explanation of how I did not particularly describe myself as Sufi, nor indeed feel the need for such labels. I would then go on to explain that although I did appreciate, and agree with the Sufi concern about the reality rather than the outward manifestation of things, in my view that did not mean that Islam advocated a shunning of this world. Monasticism played no part in Islam, which as far as I was concerned, encourages man to get involved in society, albeit with the caveat that the ultimate reality lies elsewhere, this world being merely a test. Then I would go away thinking how bizarre it was that Sufism seemed to crop up so regularly in conversation and that, often, when I was asked about it, I got the impression that the questioner was rather hoping I would say I was a Sufi. The concern I had was that there may be a particular drive in certain quarters to promote Sufism, not out of any concern for the spiritual essence of Islam, but out of an underhand attempt to depoliticize Muslims by persuading them that their faith was really an apolitical one which, if anything advocated the conscious avoidance of involvement in worldly affairs. This message would struggle to gain acceptance if it was imposed, or even suggested, from outside the community, so tactically it would need to be promoted from within.

This suspicion was only heightened when I became aware of the controversy surrounding Haris Rafiq and the Sufi Muslim Council. Once again the truth is perhaps a little blurry but what does emerge is the birth of a new Muslim organisation which had the backing of the government of the day, hardly a ringing endorsement given that government's other follies, and was seen as acting as a counter to the Muslim Council of Britain. So, for an organisation claiming to represent the "apolitical" side of Islam, it had got off to a particularly political start. It even had the former British ambassador to Uzbekistan, Craig Murray, accusing it of being linked to American neo-conservative organisations, which hardly seemed consistent with the peace-loving Sufis that it claimed to represent. In fact, there were those who made the point that genuine Sufis do not describe themselves as such anyway, preferring to concentrate privately on purifying their inner selves, rather than establishing organisations occupying a very public space. Whatever the truth may be behind this organisation, what can safely be said is that in the six or seven years it has been going, despite its suggestions that 80 per cent of British Muslims are from a Sufi background, it has hardly managed to rally them under its apolitical banner, and has fallen by the wayside much like other unrepresentative groupings before it. Government support and funding is a wonderful thing but, perhaps the lesson is that it only takes you so far.

Such examples are simply the ones that are exposed, and it hardly needs to be said that the intention behind them is surely that their origins should remain undisclosed. Muslims therefore, (and, in fact, the rest of society) need to be vigilant to the sinister games that are being played out there. To be fair, it is not only the Muslims who are the victims of such games, where things are not always how they appear to be, but for some time now, they certainly seem to have been on the receiving end more often than others.

But although a degree of scepticism is undoubtedly in order, as far as Muslims are concerned, they need to progress beyond pointing the finger at others and begin to recognise and act upon their own failings. They must avoid being gullible and reacting so predictably, so often. They need to develop a greater confidence when dealing with others, and not the confidence of simply being able to shout the loudest, which regrettably we are highly proficient at, but rather the security which comes with knowing one's position in the world, one's values, and one's purpose. The assertion of Muslim values thereafter, should not be the hollow, and often hypocritical mantra "it's against our religion" which we hear all too regularly, but in fact, should be an assertion made by actions rather than words. I imagine if we Muslims truly lived according to the values we espouse, then there would probably be very little that we would have to say, and the "Revolution Muslims" of this world would not find such receptive ears so readily.

Muslims also need to realise that they are not alone in holding certain values. There are billions of people in the world who believe in a Supreme Being, who believe that they will be held accountable for their actions in this world, and who believe that there is such a thing as morality, and that it is a force for good which needs to govern our actions. Muslims can claim no exclusivity over this. In so far as it is accurate to suggest that religion involves God as the sea and the differing religions are the rivers leading to that sea, then it may be that Muslims can claim that their river is the one, which provides the most straightforward access to the sea, with the least obstacles. Firstly, however, this does not render the other faiths as untrue or meaningless, and in fact, the Quran says as much. For example, in 2:62 of the Quran, God clearly states that those who believe in God, and the hereafter, and do good deeds, will have their reward with their Lord, and have no cause to fear. Secondly, although we may have been blessed with the clearest of tributaries leading to God, this in itself has not prevented some of us from doing our best to introduce obstacles into it and, pardon the pun, to muddy the waters. These are the perennial human failings, which have constantly added to, diluted, explained, and otherwise addressed the simple Divine commandments, and thereby introduced the man-made element into religion. This does not mean that religion itself has no basis, but just that that basis is often ignored, or departed from, and needs to be returned to and refreshed in every generation.

Once we establish that we hold certain values in common, a concerted effort needs to be made to formalise that understanding by building alliances with others. It is difficult enough to live according to certain religious values in modern society, but to do so alone is much more difficult than doing so with the support of the community around you. This applies not just to individuals but also to wider groupings. Much more would be achieved if Muslims were able to call on their counterparts in other faiths, particularly Judaism and Christianity, and show a united front. This has to start with conversations and the building of friendships as foundations. How appalling is it that relations with Jews, who at one stage in history used to seek sanctuary in Muslim countries, are at such a low ebb, that many people think that enmity has always been the defining feature of the Jewish-Muslim relationship. Efforts need to be initiated, appreciated and reciprocated.

One of my proudest moments was being asked to be a godfather/spiritual friend when my close friends, Steven and Anya, had their baby daughter. Their Christianity did not prevent them seeing qualities in me which they felt justified such a role, and then approaching their vicar to see how they could make this happen. And, happily, my Islam recognised and appreciated the friendship and love that was thereby being offered, and was thrilled to accept the invitation. And although these relationships may start on a personal level, the possibilities thereafter are endless. There is no reason why they cannot help in creating communities that are strong, yet compassionate, unified, yet diverse. The sadness often arises not between individuals, but when those with the power and influence to bring communities together, neglect their duties in achieving this potential. I still regard it as a shameful omission that the British Council, for example, can create a booklet called *Our Shared Europe* to assist with social cohesion efforts on the continent by recalling the historical contributions of Muslims in Europe, and, yet fail to see how this same publication could be such a powerful tool for bringing youngsters together in our own schools in Britain.

There are so many issues on which a common approach is warranted. Regrettably there is often a lazy assumption on the part of some Muslims that what is not obviously "Muslim" must somehow be inferior. This most often applies to social behaviour and the regarding of western culture as being defined by prejudice, drunkenness and debauchery. Not only is this hypocritical, overlooking the blatant racism and caste and tribal discrimination in many Muslim societies, coupled with levels of immorality that would make the average "infidel" blush, but it is also erroneous. It was not without good cause that an Islamic scholar once remarked upon returning to his country from the West that, "there I saw Islam but no Muslims, here I see Muslims but no Islam". He had rightly observed the implementation in Western countries of "Islamic" values such as fairness, tolerance, honesty, a lack of corruption, and welfare provision for the needy, with not a Muslim in sight. Yet when he returned to a land rich in Muslims, he found it poor in all the values that Muslims should stand for. We need to move beyond an understanding of morality, which restricts itself to personal (usually sexual) behaviour, whilst ignoring the incessant corruption evident in much of our governance.

There are also many areas in which Muslims can learn from others who have already had to grapple with reconciling religious belief with the demands of modern life and can now share their experiences and knowledge with others. Just as a thousand years ago many non-Muslims benefited from knowledge which was in the hands of Muslims, so too, Muslims now need to realise that they can similarly benefit from others without this meaning an inevitable dilution of their own beliefs. They can find those who share their values and tackle together the many difficulties that are faced by society today. When the bankers ran off with taxpayers' money, they could not have cared less if the bailout came from a Muslim, Christian or atheist source. Similarly when "austerity" measures are imposed by governments seeking to placate the world of finance, they do not discriminate between believer and non-believer. These and other pressing social issues need to be tackled by those with the expertise to do so, and the wider this grouping, the more chance it has of success.

In so far as Muslims become involved in such tasks, as they should, they need to do this without resorting to the dogmatic approach to faith, which no longer works, and in any event was never supposed to be the Islamic way. In addressing these concerns together with others, they can hope to recreate the success story of Cordoba a thousand years ago. They can attempt to create a society where there is mutual co-operation for mutual benefit; a society that does not have such a gulf between the haves and have-nots; a society where tolerance means more than simply putting up with each other; in short, a society which should be the norm in modern Western states, but sadly is becoming more of a distant prospect with the passing of each day.

The day after the 7/7 bombings in London, I was asked to do Pause for Thought on BBC Radio 2. I was as appalled and upset as the next person at what had happened, and certainly did not think that I had any great insights to offer, but after some hesitation, I agreed. I spoke of being united in grief with the rest of the nation, my nation. I made it clear that I followed Islam and prayed five times a day. But then I also checked the Liverpool FC website five times a day too. What defined me, however, was my humanity.

At the time I was the Chair of the Merseyside Council of Faiths which received a letter from an English lady who had listened to that particular Pause for Thought, and felt compelled to write to commend me on what I had said, and remark that it had made her feel "proud" that I was British. I found her comments uplifting but the fact remained, I had done nothing special. I was, after all, just your average Muslim.

Suggested Further Reading

Islam, A Short History – **Karen Armstrong**

Muhammad – **Karen Armstrong**

Muhammad – **Martin Lings**

How Islam Created the Modern World – **Mark Graham**

Light From the East – **John Freely**

The House of Wisdom – **Jonathon Lyons**

The Eastern Origins of Western Civilisation – **John Hobson**

Lost History – **Michael Morgan**

The Alchemy of Happiness – **Al-Ghazali**

*The Reconstruction of Religious
Thought in Islam* – **M. Iqbal**

The Heart of Islam – **SeyyedHossain Nasr**

Progressive Muslims – **Omid Safi**

Desperately Seeking Paradise – **Zia Sardar**

Interpreting the Quran – **Abdullah Saeed**

No God But God – **Reza Aslan**

The Great Theft – **KhaledAbou El Fadl**

Inside the Gender Jihad – **Amina Wadud**

Quran and Woman – **Amina Wadud**

On Being Muslim – **Farid Esack**

Who Needs an Islamic State – **A. El-Affendi**

Jinnah, Pakistan and Islamic Identity – **Akbar Ahmed**

The Ornament of the World – **Maria Menocal**

A Short History of Nearly Everything – **Bill Bryson**

The Best Democracy Money Can Buy – **Greg Palast**

The Problem With Interest – **Tarek El Diwany**

Interest in Islamic Economics – **Abdulkader Thomas**

Confessions of an Economic Hitman – **John Perkins**

Deterring Democracy – **Noam Chomsky**

The Fateful Triangle – **Noam Chomsky**

The Shock Doctrine – **Naomi Klein**

Rogue State – **William Blum**

Perpetual War for Perpetual Peace – **Gore Vidal**

Wrestling With Zion – **Kushner and Solomon**

Arabs and Israel for Beginners – **Ron David**

Lightning Source UK Ltd.
Milton Keynes UK
UKOW05f2103160114

224761UK00001B/10/P